NOTES ON SCHUBERT

NOTES ON SCHUBERT

20 Crucial Works

Conrad Wilson

William B. Eerdmans Publishing Company
Grand Rapids, Michigan

59548826

To Nick and Susie, who have heard a lot of it

© 2003 Conrad Wilson

First published 2003 by Saint Andrew Press, Edinburgh

This edition published 2005
in the United States of America by
Wm. B. Eerdmans Publishing Company
255 Jefferson Ave. S.E., Grand Rapids, Michigan 49503

Printed in the United States of America

10 09 08 07 06 05   7 6 5 4 3 2 1

ISBN 0–8028–2928–7

www.eerdmans.com

CONTENTS

Foreword   vii

Introduction   1

1   'Gretchen am Spinnrade', D118   7

2   Symphony No. 3 in D major, D200   15

3   Piano Quintet in A major ('The Trout'), D667   19

4   Symphony No. 7 (8) in B minor ('Unfinished'), D759   24

5   *Wanderer Fantasy*, D760   28

6   *Die schöne Müllerin*, D795   33

7   Octet in F major, D803   40

8   String Quartet in A minor, D804   47

9   Piano Sonata in D major, D850   53

10	Symphony No. 8 (9) in C major ('Great'), D944	57
11	String Quartet in D minor ('Death and the Maiden'), D810	62
12	String Quartet in G major, D887	67
13	Four Impromptus, D899; Four Impromptus, D935	72
14	Piano Trio in E flat major, D929	77
15	*Winterreise*, D911	83
16	Fantasy in F minor for piano duet, D940	90
17	Piano Sonata in A major, D959	95
18	Piano Sonata in B flat major, D960	100
19	String Quintet in C major, D956	105
20	*Schwanengesang*, D957	111
	Further Listening	117
	Further Reading	120
	Glossary	122

FOREWORD

Why twenty? Obviously it is a device, one way of drawing attention to some of the masterpieces in a great composer's output. But at the same time it is a discipline and a challenge. Why choose these particular works and not others? The question and its answers are my reason for writing this book and its companions on other composers. In making my selection, I thought twenty works to be a good, sufficiently tight number. Increase it to thirty and choice becomes easier, perhaps too easy. Reduce it to ten and, in the case of great productive composers, you don't really have enough music wholly to justify what you are doing. Too many crucial works would have to be excluded, and the gaps would be glaring. So twenty it is, though not in the sense of a top twenty, because a crucial work does not actually have to be a great one, and the works are not listed – how could they be? – in any order of merit.

But each of them, it seems to me, needs to mark a special moment in its composer's life – perhaps a turning point, perhaps a sudden flash of inspiration, perhaps an intensifying of genius, as when Schubert produced his setting of Goethe's 'Gretchen am Spinnrade' at the age of 17, or Mozart his G major Violin Concerto, K216, at 19, or Beethoven his C minor Piano Trio, Op. 1, No. 3, at 25.

None of these composers was a prodigy as gifted as Mendelssohn, whose String Octet and whose *A Midsummer Night's Dream* overture were the most astounding teenage masterpieces of all time. But if there was nothing so arresting to be found among Mozart's or Schubert's numerous boyhood works, the change when it came was startling.

With Schubert's first great song, Mozart's first great concerto and Beethoven's first great piece of chamber music came the shock of surprise in the form of an audacious new command of melody and accompaniment, a conspicuous leap in quality and, in the slow movement of the Mozart, a grasp of the mystery of beauty which made his two previous violin concertos, written in the same year, seem blandly impersonal exercises in composition.

Yet this third of Mozart's five violin concertos is not a masterpiece in the sense that *Don Giovanni* is, just as Schubert's boyhood String Quartet in E flat major, D87, for all its melodic beauty, is not as overwhelming as 'Death and the Maiden'. Nor, for that matter, does Beethoven's Second Symphony possess the size and sustaining power of his Third, the 'Eroica', though it has unquestionable excitements of its own.

It is not the aim of these books to set one masterpiece against another, or to suggest that early works are automatically less interesting than late ones. To regard a composer's output purely as a process of evolution is to fail inexcusably to accept a work on its own terms – a serious flaw in assessments of Schubert, who, according to many a pundit, did not 'find' himself until he was almost dead.

So, early works are not being banned from these pages, even if it means the loss of some late ones. Nor is my decision to deal with the music chronologically based on any intrinsic belief that it reflects in some special way a composer's progress. The intention is simply to shed light on what was happening to him at the time he wrote a particular piece, where he was, what he was doing or experiencing, and how the music fits into the general pattern of his life and output. To go beyond this, by claiming that Haydn, for example, 'progressed' from his *Storm and Stress* symphonies to his *London* ones, or Mozart from his E flat major Piano Concerto, K271, to his E flat major, K482, is to undervalue his achievement as a whole.

So, no masterpiece has been omitted simply because its composer later in some way surpassed it. Some works are included simply because I adore them, or am prepared to defend them against the judgement of people who detest them. Liking a piece of music, we should always remember, is not the opposite of disliking it. It is a different condition altogether, and being able to explain why we like it is perhaps more important in the end than pronouncing on whether it is good music or bad.

Each of these twenty short essays is a species of what are traditionally known as programme notes – the descriptions to be found in printed concert or opera programmes of what is being performed that night. Donald Francis Tovey, one-time professor of music at Edinburgh University, was a famed and erudite pioneer of the form in the early twentieth century, and his collected *Essays in Musical Analysis* remain good to read, even if their style now seems old-fashioned and out of tune with today's musical thinking. Nor are they always accurate. Scholarship has progressed since Tovey's time.

Nevertheless, what Tovey wrote still towers over much of what passes for programme notes today. Even during my own post-Tovey boyhood, programme notes incorporated – as Tovey's did – musical examples because it was assumed that concert-goers could read music. Today, such notes would be branded elitist. To include musical terminology at all tends to be frowned upon. I have been asked why, in my own notes, I employ such terms as 'counterpoint', which nobody understands. But are football correspondents similarly chided for writing 'penalty' or 'free kick'? Somehow I think not. Though I am all against jargon, the use of an established, accessible musical term is preferable to a paragraph of explanation.

Concert programmes are now a dumbed-down art in which fatuous puffs about the performers occupy more space than the notes themselves, and adverts are given more space still. Traditional notes, as the chief executive of a concert organisation has remarked to me, are now 'irrelevant'. In the sense that most concerts today take place in darkened halls, he was perhaps right. But notes are written to be read before and after an event, as well as during it, and this book's intention is to fill that need.

In the sixteen years I spent editing the Edinburgh Festival's programme notes, there were a number of house rules which I worked out with the then Festival director, Peter Diamand, whose European outlook differed from, and was refreshingly less 'commercial' than, the British. Diamand's beliefs, which I shared, were that notes should contain facts rather than flimflam; that speculation was acceptable so long as it was informed; that notes should be coherently devised by a single writer for the contents of a single programme; that connections between one work and another should be mentioned; that the author, as Tovey once decreed, should act as counsel for the defence – Diamand detested notes which gave the impression that 'This is a bad work but let's perform it anyway'; and that artists' biographies should be confined to 150 words, should include no adjectives and should supply no information about what a performer would be performing in future seasons.

Though most of these principles have fallen by the wayside, they are still the ones to which I, as a note-writer, would prefer to adhere. In addition, I would say that, wherever possible, a work's place in musical history needs to be established; that its local connections (if any) should be mentioned; and that the writer has a responsibility to lure the reader into the music.

Some of the notes included in these pages are based on notes originally written for one musical organisation or another, but which have gone through a constant process of change, and which have now been changed yet again to suit the needs of a book about a single great composer. No note, whether for a concert programme or for something more permanent, should be merely 'drawn from stock'. Just as every performance of a work forms a part (however small) of that work's history, so every programme note should reflect the state – and status – of that work at the time the annotator is writing about it. Attitudes alter. Here, in this book, are twenty current attitudes (my own, but also quoting those of others) to twenty works that continue to matter.

Finally, a note on format. Each book begins with a fresh assessment of its subject composer and of the way he is performed at the start of the twenty-first century. Books are listed for further reading, and technical terms are explained in a brief glossary. Recordings are recommended at the end of each short essay, with record numbers provided wherever possible. Since prices vary from shop to shop, it seems sensible simply to generalise, saying where a disc, or set of discs, is bargain-price or otherwise at the time of going to press.

CONRAD WILSON
Edinburgh, 2003

INTRODUCTION

More than two centuries after his birth, Schubert is being reassessed. His greatness no longer seems on a lower level than Mozart's or Beethoven's. His areas of genius have widened to include more than his songs, a symphony or two, a few pieces of chamber music, and the piano *morceaux* for which he has always been loved. Even his piano sonatas, long dismissed as prolix and maladroit, are recognised as the masterpieces they are.

But what of Schubert the man? Though the sentimentalised *Blossom Time* depiction of him has long since receded, there are still large areas of his personality we can only guess at. He left far fewer letters than Mozart, and they are often less communicative than those of his great predecessor. He travelled less, and was not much of a public figure, except in bars and at parties mostly attended by people his own age. He was no great pianist, and did not give high-profile performances the way Beethoven and Mozart did. He was not a conductor, the way Mendelssohn and Berlioz would soon be, and as the deaf Beethoven did his best to be. We do not even know for sure if he ever met Beethoven, whose path he must have crossed many times in Vienna. He has been called an eternal student with no fixed address, though the description hardly fits the composer of the 'Great' C major Symphony.

Yet, in spite of the shortage of facts, a picture – or study in contrasts – has gradually emerged. Was he sociable or solitary? Manic-depressive or merely moody? Amiable or given to rages? Straight or gay? A dramatist or a lyricist? Current thinking is that he was all of these things, and to insist that he was one or another is to suppress a vital element of his make-up. Yet people do not like their comfortable picture of a merry (as opposed to 'gay') Schubert to be in any way disturbed or disfigured.

The supreme untroubled melodist, warbling his woodnotes wild, inspired by babbling brooks, carving his beloved's name on every tree, scribbling songs on the backs of menus, is a vision hard to dislodge, and one into which the sombre Schubert, locking himself into his room in the expectation that he might be dead by morning, does not quite fit. Even the American musicologist Maynard Solomon's cautious exploration of the composer's sexual nature in *Schubert and the Peacocks of Benvenuto Cellini* – which is not quite so startling or as new as it seems – was quite intemperately attacked in some quarters. Yet, more than sixty years ago, the famous record-producer Walter Legge – husband of Elisabeth Schwarzkopf, one of the greatest exponents of Schubert's songs – claimed that the composer's homosexuality had always been known about in Vienna.

The question is whether it matters. Does our knowledge of this possibility throw fresh light on his music? If it does so in the case of Benjamin Britten — and it certainly does — then the same can surely be said for Schubert. The orchestral and instrumental works may or may not remain as they were (see the note on the 'Unfinished' symphony later in this book), but the songs shift ground. Songs, after all, have texts, chosen by the composer for reasons that may be quite specific, or implied, or submerged.

Is it surprising that Schubert's dark settings of poems by his homosexual and suicidal friend, Johann Mayrhofer, are being examined anew? What does his lovely but (dare one say?) camp treatment of Goethe's 'Ganymed' — a song Britten especially loved — tell us about his sexuality? What is the truth behind *Die schöne Müllerin*, and is it purely fanciful to suggest, as some commentators now do, that the stream which flows through this song cycle, and ultimately drowns the miller's lad, symbolises Schubert's homosexual yearnings?

The sheer beauty of Schubert's music can be disarming, concealing the morbid undercurrents which Bernard Levin, in an admiring essay, once completely failed to perceive in the great C major String Quintet. Fritz Lehner's penetrating East German film, *Mit meinen heissen Tränen* ('With My Burning Tears'), also known as *Notturno*, came nearer the heart of the matter, drawing attention to the grimmer, sadder, more obsessive and alienated composer than the amiable songsmith depicted in Schubert fiction.

Even a song as airily lilting as 'Seligkeit' ('Happiness'), we can now discern, is not really happy at all. Though Schwarzkopf sang it with sparkling sweetness and youthfulness, a more modern recording by Brigitte Fassbaender paints a different picture. It is not just that Fassbaender's mezzo voice casts a darker light on music to which Schwarzkopf brought exquisite soprano sheen, but that it presents happiness in true Schubertian terms as something questionable and transitory. The disc's cover shows Fassbaender sitting in a graveyard, as much a tribute to 'Seligkeit' as to 'Death and the Maiden', which is also included.

No doubt we all continue to get out of Schubert's music only what we put into it. The authorities who used to patronise his fecundity – 'if only he had spent more time reconsidering what he had written' – are all now dead. The works remain. The people who used to find the symphonies and string quartets 'immature', the products of a composer who died too soon, no longer prattle so much about every Schubert work being an early work. Grillparzer's famous posthumous inscription – that Schubert left behind 'a rich treasure but still fairer hopes' – can now be seen for the well-intentioned nonsense it is.

With this has come the belated recognition that Schubert was seldom if ever inept. His piano sonatas, once deemed maladroit, prolix and tiring to play, now stand beside Beethoven's in their mastery. His Viennese dance music, all those sequences of piano pieces, remain small marvels of inspiration (which in turn inspired Johann Strauss and others), and seem all the more remarkable when we remember that Schubert himself never danced.

Being only five feet tall, tinier than Toulouse-Lautrec, Schubert perhaps feared that he would look ridiculous on the dance floor. At the keyboard, however, he sat shoulder to shoulder with his listeners. It was in packed rooms, rather than in spacious halls, that he was in his element, and it was in such surroundings that his not-always-accurate playing must have shone. Sometimes he sang to his own accompaniment – hard to imagine Brahms doing that – yet he was no dilettante. He was a musician of passionate seriousness, whose association, somewhat claustrophobic, with what in Germany is known as 'house music' was not invariably to his benefit. Only when it eventually got out of the house, and into the wider world, did Schubert's music really prosper.

Finally, a note on numbering. All works described in these pages are identified by their 'D' numbers, drawn from Otto Erich Deutsch's painstaking catalogue of Schubert's works. Since 1951, this has been the standard method of Schubert identification, replacing the old and inaccurate opus numbers, some of which (such as Op. 100 for the E flat major Piano Trio) have proved hard to dislodge.

NOTES ON SCHUBERT

Haydn, Mozart, Beethoven and Brahms became residents of Vienna, but only Franz Schubert was born there. The place was a house called The Red Crayfish, now a museum, on Nussdorfer Strasse, with a quiet inner courtyard. The date was 31 January 1797. Haydn, in his mid-sixties, and Beethoven, aged 27, had by then settled in the city, and Mozart had died there six years earlier. Never before, and never again, would there be so great a concentration of high musical genius in a single area.

Schubert, a schoolmaster's son, was one of fourteen children, only five of whom survived to adulthood. The Schubert home doubled as the father's school, which he ran successfully enough to require larger premises by 1801. They were an educated family, and a musical one, though not so musical, or so musically ambitious, as the Mozarts. But with their father's encouragement – he himself was a cellist – the children all learned to play instruments. A family string quartet was formed, with young Franz as viola-player, and out of this grew a chamber orchestra with the support of friends and neighbours.

Though more modest than Mozart, Schubert was a choirboy by the age of 8. At 11 he won a scholarship to the Imperial and Royal Chapel, where Salieri, the Kapellmeister, taught him counterpoint. His education, both musical and general, was assured. While there, he befriended Josef von Spaun, a law student and musical enthusiast who held a wake for him when he died. His compositions, once he had started composing, came thick and fast, and would continue to do so for the rest of his life.

One

1814
'GRETCHEN AM SPINNRADE', D118

'Gretchen at the Spinning Wheel' was where it all began. Composed at 17, it was not the first of Schubert's 600-or-so songs. The quiet trainee schoolteacher, who had been a less ostentatious *wunderkind* than Mozart and a less phenomenal one than Mendelssohn, already had a mountain of music to his credit. But 'Gretchen' was his first Goethe song, and it was his first great song. In the year he produced it, he had attended the premiere of Beethoven's final version of *Fidelio* in Vienna, had completed the ninth of his fifteen string quartets, and would start work on the second of his eight symphonies. It was 'Gretchen', however, which marked the dividing line between Schubert the boy and the ageless composer who would be posthumously hailed by Liszt as 'the most poetic of all musicians'.

For novice listeners, Schubert's songs form the easiest way into his music, most of them being short, characteristic, based on comprehensible poetic ideas, and with memorable melodies. But the sheer volume of them – from his boyhood portrayal of a child's funeral ('A Corpse Fantasy',

D10, based on Schiller) to the airily pastoral 'Shepherd on the Rock', written just before his death – can seem daunting. Some of them, not many, add to the confusion by being different settings of the same poem. Others, seemingly designed for men, may be sung by women, and vice versa. But with so vast an output, attracting so many performers, such contradictions are bound to occur. Aspiring singers always want to sing Schubert, and it is easy to see why.

In public performance, a Schubert song seldom stands alone. It forms part of a Schubert group, or of an entire Schubert recital in which the songs may be variously categorised – by date of composition, by choice of poet, by mood or subject matter, or simply by contrast. Schubert drew inspiration from poets as great as Goethe or as unknown as Count Leopold Stolberg, whose name survives almost exclusively through Schubert's setting of 'Auf dem Wasser zu singen', that blissfully flowing water idyll in which we encounter the essence – one essence – of Schubert.

He could, as is traditionally said, be attracted to good poets or bad. It all depended on whether a text spoke music to him. The fact that 'Hark! Hark! The Lark!', by a good poet called William Shakespeare, spoke music so urgently to him that he dashed off the song on the back of a menu was just one of many false impressions given of Schubert as an impulsive, 'natural' composer, scribbling the first thing that came into his head. He was not like that at all. Likewise, his taste was more consistently good than it has been made out to be, even though he was perfectly capable of producing a great song from unworthy material. In song, as in opera, the composer (to quote Joseph Kerman's famous dictum) is the dramatist.

Many Schubert songs were based on poems by friends. Many, too, were originally sung by friends, or even by Schubert himself at house parties and inns around Vienna. These gatherings came to be known as Schubertiads, cosy, convivial occasions, often male-dominated, in which nothing was too rigidly organised and new songs could be heard alongside new versions of old ones. Today's Schubert recitals, whether given in a formal concert hall or at home via a bundle of CD recordings, are the direct descendants of Schubert's own Schubertiads.

As Schubert's main outlets for his latest songs, however, Schubertiads were serious as well as social events. His enthusiasm for Goethe resulted in seventy-four songs, thirty of them written in a single year. Schiller inspired more than forty, the melancholy Mayrhofer nearly fifty. The famous story that Schubert sent a batch of twenty songs to Goethe in Weimar, and that the poet sent them straight back without acknowledgement, is not strictly true. The songs were indeed sent to Goethe, but by Schubert's friend Josef von Spaun, whose accompanying letter was so fulsome that Goethe could only have been repelled by it.

Yet Schubert's Goethe settings were in a different class from those of Mozart or Beethoven, composers who had the poet's seal of approval. Theirs were simply songs, albeit fine ones, whereas Schubert's went further in the way they fused melody with declamation, voice with accompaniment.

With Schubert, singer and pianist for the first time became equal partners. The piano part was as important as the vocal line, and often startlingly different from it – as in 'Gretchen', where the piano represents the incessant sound of the spinning wheel. It does more than that, however. It evokes Gretchen's obsessive love for Faust, just as the eternal sound of the stream in *Die schöne Müllerin* would later underpin the miller lad's imagined relationship with the miller's daughter. Only when Gretchen recalls Faust's kiss – a moment of high drama in the song – does the sound of the spinning wheel abruptly cease.

When Schubert completed 'Gretchen' on 19 October 1814, the German *Lied*, or 'art-song', was born. Significantly, Schubert supplied the exact date, as if he knew, even at the age of 17, that it should be commemorated. Songwriting was no longer a sideline for a great composer, as it had been for Haydn and Mozart and still was for Beethoven. Songs, for Schubert, were as important as sonatas and string quartets. They would soon be for Schumann as well, and, even more so, for Hugo Wolf, who devoted his entire career to song.

No recorded performance of 'Gretchen' delivers Faust's kiss more fiercely than Elisabeth Schwarzkopf's with Edwin Fischer as pianist – a great musical partnership if ever there was one. Schwarzkopf's style, by today's standards, is undoubtedly 'mannered', and you will either love it or loathe it – modern singers would prefer a purer delivery. But it is part of musical history, and the entire recital, including eleven other indispensable Schubert songs, along with Fischer's solo account of the six *Moments Musicaux*, is an enthralling experience (EMI CDH5 67494-2). Disappointingly, Janet Baker fudges Faust's kiss in an otherwise exemplary two-disc compilation, mostly with Gerald Moore as pianist (EMI CDS5 69389-2).

Other collections of primary interest are two by Christophe Prégardien, the best of modern Schubert tenors. The first focuses on songs of travel and farewell, those potently interlinked Schubert subjects (Virgin 7243 5 61912 2 8), the second on settings of Mayrhofer, Schubert's troubled friend, with whom he resided for some years and who proved deeply influential, both musically and personally, on the young composer. The latter disc has an added interest in that the accompaniment, played by Andreas Staier, employs an authentically light-toned Schubertian fortepiano (Teldec 8573-85556-2). Bryn Terfel's magisterial baritone recital with Malcolm Martineau has 'Erlkönig', one of the greatest of the early Goethe settings, as a searing highlight (DG 445 294-2).

Each of these recordings is in a class of its own. Even more so are two lavishly comprehensive Schubert sets. Dietrich Fischer-Dieskau's, containing every Schubert song suitable for male voice, comes on twenty-one discs in three cut-price boxes with Gerald Moore as pianist. Volume One contains 234 early songs, Volume Two a further 171 from 1817 onwards, and Volume Three gathers the song sets *Die schöne Müllerin*, *Winterreise* and *Schwanengesang*. When he recorded them, between 1966 and 1972, Fischer-

Dieskau was in his finest voice, bringing meticulous articulation, keen intelligence and exquisite beauty of baritone tone to the entire collection (DG 437 215-2, 437 225-2 and 437 235-2).

The pianist Stephen Johnson, even more ambitiously, has collected Schubert's entire output of songs on the thirty-seven discs of his 'Hyperion Schubert Edition'. Employing a different singer or singers for each disc, invariably with himself as pianist, he provides a fascinating, truly Schubertian journey through the music. Most of the discs are solo recitals, but some come as Schubertiads featuring groups of singers. Though the quality inevitably varies, the overall standard is high and in some cases (Christophe Prégardien, Christine Schäfer, Matthias Goerne, Brigitte Fassbaender, Felicity Lott, Peter Schreier, Edith Mathis and Ann Murray, to name but eight) more than that.

The discs come separately, each with texts, translations and lengthy, detailed notes by Johnson, which put many other Schubert collections to shame. The more recent issues, moreover, are supplied in sturdy boxes, far superior to the standard CD plastic containers. Too numerous to list by number, these are discs to collect one by one, and to savour.

Schubert composed eight symphonies, one of them (not the last) famously unfinished, and two of them wrongly numbered. At the start of the twenty-first century, the inaccuracy seems slovenly but typical of the innumerable false beliefs about Schubert. Why nobody has bothered to correct the numbering, least of all performers and concert-promoters, is nevertheless easy to understand. Since nine has become an emotive symphonic symbol — Beethoven, Dvořák, Bruckner and the superstitious Mahler each produced nine symphonies before dying — the morbid misconception that Schubert, too, was one of the group has become just another part of Schubert mythology.

But there is more to it than that. What actually counts as a Schubert symphony, and what does not, remains a subject for debate. The 'Unfinished' is in fact one of several unfinished Schubert symphonies, but it is the only one which is capable of being performed the way Schubert left it. The others all require the services of arrangers, orchestrators, transcribers, tamperers, plastic surgeons, spiritualists, opportunists and other interventionists. But the difference between true Schubert and mock-Schubert needs to be clearly defined, which is one reason for proper numbering and identification.

Since the so-called Symphony No. 7 in E major is little more than an outline sketch, which Schubert for unstated reasons decided to abandon, it seems hardly to deserve an official slot between the thoroughly authentic Symphony No. 6 and the 'Unfinished', traditionally but erroneously known as No. 8. It is the 'Unfinished' which should be called Symphony No. 7, transforming the 'Great' C major Symphony into No. 8 rather than leaving it as No. 9. This is the numbering refreshingly *followed by the meticulous Viennese conductor, Nikolaus Harnoncourt, in his complete recording of the symphonies based on the New Schubert Edition, though whether anybody will follow suit remains to be seen.*

But Schubert's symphonies have always been problematic, in terms of correctly detailed editions as well as matters of identification. For years, there was a much-discussed 'lost' Schubert symphony, known as the 'Gastein', because that was where he was believed to have written part of it. Then it turned out that the 'Gastein' symphony was really the 'Great' C major, and the problem ceased to exist.

A further enigma surrounded the huge and splendid 'Grand Duo' for piano duet, another work which has come to be identified, quite gratuitously, as the Symphony No. 7. Was this magnificent four-handed sonata Schubert's own keyboard arrangement of a symphony whose orchestral parts had vanished? Schumann, who knew the piano version, claimed to hear an orchestra behind every note. Brahms, who held similar views, persuaded the violinist Joseph Joachim to orchestrate it in order to let people hear how it was meant to sound. The Edinburgh-based Schubert authority, Sir Donald Tovey, gave his blessing to the orchestration by affirming that the piano version had never seemed very pianistic to him. But there was a time when people said such things about most of Schubert's piano works — and the 'Grand Duo' turned out to be a piano duet after all, the greatest ever written.

Two

1815
SYMPHONY NO. 3 IN D MAJOR, D200

Adagio maestoso – Allegro con brio   Allegretto

Menuetto: Vivace   Presto vivace

Schubert experts tend to speak ill of his early symphonies. But if the 'Unfinished', composed at the age of 25, is more than just another early Schubert symphony, and if the 'Great' C major, which he began the following year, is more still, what are we to say about that brilliant teenage feat of compression, the Symphony No. 3, written during the summer of 1815? Clearly, it is not a mature masterpiece in the same sense as these two later works; but a masterpiece it undoubtedly is, driven by the same sort of irresistible energy as would propel the finale of his last completed symphony, the 'Great' C major, to its close.

Yet even to hail it as a stepping stone on the way to that vast and tremendous outpouring of genius is scarcely enough, for the Symphony No. 3 is tremendous in its own right, its only possible shortcoming being that it does not go quite so far. Yet the distance it travels, from the ominously hammered-out sonorities of the slow introduction right through to the swerving energy of the tarantella-like finale, is surely sufficient to guarantee its success. In a good performance – which is one that reveals this symphony to be more than a mere prentice piece – the thrust of its first movement and finale should be like a galvanic force, unimpeded by the sweetness of the slow movement (which is a short and lightweight allegretto rather than a full-blown andante or adagio) or by the bouncingly jovial minuet.

Schubert's Symphony No. 3 could be described as a domestic symphony, though not in the same sense as Richard Strauss's *Sinfonia Domestica*. It is not about the home life of the Schuberts, though it comes quite close to that by being written for a neighbourhood orchestra, which had steadily grown from a family string quartet – with young Schubert himself as viola-player – into something considerably larger, comprising about twenty strings, plus woodwind, brass and drums. These players gathered regularly to perform new music *chez* Schubert or (as gradually became necessary) in larger premises owned by friends and acquaintances.

By the time he was 18, Schubert was already a prolific composer. Of the 1,000-or-so pieces he had produced by the end of his short life, more than half were written before he was 21. But though his first symphonies were based on Viennese symphonic tradition as he knew it – with Haydn, Mozart and Beethoven among his models – their flavour was original and already recognisably Schubertian, so much so that the main theme of the first movement of the Third Symphony is almost identical to that of the first movement of the 'Great' C major.

Yet, supreme melodist though he was, Schubert knew that symphonic themes did not have to be melodic – this one is conspicuously confined to rhythm and harmony, and is in no obvious way 'tuneful'. But melody certainly asserts itself in the slow movement, with its gently ambling opening theme on strings and woodwind, followed by an even more engaging one on clarinet. The minuet, fast enough to be a Beethoven scherzo, is characterised by its leaping offbeat accents and its songlike trio section, with prominent woodwind. The racy finale, like the first movement, sticks almost entirely to a single extended melody – a hurtling dance of a sort Schubert would employ later, to even more obsessive effect, in his two last string quartets, 'Death and the Maiden' and the G major, D887.

Schubert's symphonies form his main body of orchestral music. Concertos lay outside his range of enthusiasms, which tended more towards intimacy – the sound of a chamber ensemble, a solo piano, a human voice – than loud demonstrations of virtuosity. For anyone wanting to explore the eight symphonies as an entity, Harnoncourt's cut-price four-disc set with the Royal Concertgebouw Orchestra, recorded in 1992, is the one to go for. He imposes the Schubert sound on the Dutch players, giving it a pungency and responsiveness to the darker undertones of the music which other performances often lack. Based on cleaned-up modern versions of the scores, the performances are incisive and never too heavy, with no glaring disparity between the treatment of the Third Symphony and that of the 'Great' C major (Teldec 4509-91184-2).

Claudio Abbado's rival set with the Chamber Orchestra of Europe, dating from 1989, is more romantic, more charming, more beautiful, and a good deal less interesting. But it has a similarly welcome lightness of touch (compare it with Herbert von Karajan and the Berlin Philharmonic), and it incorporates the 'Grand Duo' in Joachim's orchestration of it as Symphony No. 7. Since the discs are available separately, the Third Symphony can be bought in a coupling with the Fourth (DG 423 653-2). Sir Thomas Beecham's classic performance of the Third with the Royal Philharmonic, which in those days contained the cream of British wind players, would be more alluring if it were not so bottom-heavy in sound. But, if you can put up with this, the inclusion of the Fifth and Sixth symphonies makes it a super-bargain (EMI CDMS 66984-2).

Three

1819
PIANO QUINTET IN A MAJOR ('THE TROUT'), D667

Allegro vivace   Andante   Scherzo: Presto

Tema: Andantino – Variazioni I–V – Allegretto   Allegro giusto

Is it a piano trio to which two extra string players have been added? Or is it a species of string quartet into which a pianist has been infiltrated? Either way, the inclusion of a double bass in the 'Trout' quintet may seem quaint, giving its five divertimento-like movements a casual, domestic, attractively offbeat air, reflecting the circumstances in which it came to be written in the autumn of 1819, when its composer was just 22 years old.

Schubert's 'Trout', as we have come to call it, is nothing if not sociable music. In some ways, it is a lavish and natural extension of the sets of piano dances and other entertainment pieces he had written and would continue to write for the rest of his career. But it is also a melodious summing-up of his carefree youth, one of the few wholly happy large-scale works he ever wrote, dating from when he still felt at ease with the world and was untroubled by the depressions and illnesses, along with the combined effects of excessive smoking and drinking, that would soon begin to darken his personality.

The music had its inspiration in a walking tour in which Schubert was joined by his lofty baritone friend Johann Vogl – thirty years his senior – who had created the role of the sadistic Pizarro in Beethoven's *Fidelio* in Vienna five years earlier and would later, with some difficulty, sing *Winterreise*. It was a time when Schubert could still say: 'All is well with me. I live and compose like a god, as if it had to be so.' Their journey took them into the Austrian Alps, a stop being made en route at Steyr, Vogl's birthplace, a town noted for its fishing facilities. Schubert was delighted with the countryside and remarked in a letter that it was 'inconceivably lovely'. Moreover, in his guest house there lived five girls, and in the house next door another three. 'Eight girls,' he exclaimed, 'and nearly all pretty.'

It was in that idyllic atmosphere – though his attitude to the girls remains unclear – that the 'Trout' quintet was planned. During his stay at Steyr, the young composer met a local amateur musician called Sylvester Paumgartner, who had money, a cello and a fondness for Schubert's song, 'Die Forelle' ('The Trout'), written two years previously. Paumgartner had been practising Hummel's Piano Quintet with some friends, and was looking for something else that employed the same unusual combination of instruments. Such a work proving elusive, Schubert was invited to write one – and the result was the 'Trout' quintet, completed after he returned to Vienna and containing, in tribute to Paumgartner, a set of variations based on 'Die Forelle'.

It has been said that the Steyr countryside was as much the composer of this quintet as Schubert himself – and indeed, of all his instrumental works, it is the most serenely pastoral in mood, a series of sunny landscapes with occasional plunges into shadow. If you wish to introduce somebody to the world of chamber music, this is surely the work with which to do so. If you feel like switching off the CD-player and performing some chamber music yourself, this again is a work to try, provided you have the right group of instrumentalists and a better cellist than poor Paumgartner, who after all his trouble found his part too difficult.

Of the five movements, the first contains the main dramatic business of what is otherwise a relaxed and merry score. Though laid out in conventional sonata form, with a recapitulation which is almost a straight repeat of the exposition, it never descends into dullness. Schubert, even at this early stage in his career, raised repetition to the level of genius, through the use on this occasion of a leaping arpeggio on the piano, some whizzing scales, a wealth of vivacious melody, and one marvellous quiet passage which, in the middle of the movement, erupts into something suddenly louder and more passionate.

If the next movement similarly depends on repetition – the first sixty bars, it has been pointed out, are just the same as the second sixty, apart from a change of key – the result is entirely Schubertian, and repeating a passage in a different key is in any case among his most magical fingerprints. The music, in his most lilting vein, incorporates some filigree detail in the piano's upper register – another special Schubert keyboard characteristic, sometimes described as the 'crystal chandelier effect'.

The succeeding scherzo, with its quick bouncing rhythm which so disconcerts the deaf concert pianist who is the heroine of Vikram Seth's novel *An Equal Music*, again has the piano sparkling aloft, though the central trio section is more subdued. The fourth movement, with its rippling figuration and (in the allegretto coda) its vivid leaps, brings on the trout. Each instrumentalist is allowed a substantial bite of it in the course of the five variations which follow the opening statement of the D major theme. The big moment comes with the fifth variation's sudden switch to B flat major, which again shows what Schubert could achieve through a simple change of key.

The finale, with its Hungarian verve, adds a spicy dash of paprika to this five-course banquet. Such sidesteps into the Hungarian style come as a reminder of the close connections between Vienna and Hungary, celebrated in works ranging from Haydn's *Gypsy Rondo* to Johann Strauss's *Die Fledermaus*.

Schubert's Hungarian streak, audible in a number of his piano pieces, his A minor String Quartet, and the finale of his late, great C major String Quintet, was to catch the attention of a devoted Schubertian, Johannes

Brahms, almost as soon as he settled in Vienna. It influenced his *Liebeslieder Waltzes*, written in 1874, in the same way as it inspired Liszt's *Hungarian Rhapsodies*, which would never have been written but for the Hungarian composer's decision to make a solo piano arrangement of Schubert's four-handed *Hungarian Divertissement*.

There are several irresistible recordings of the 'Trout' which, with some difficulty, can be whittled down to two. Alfred Brendel's fastidiously conversational 1994 account of it with the fascinating Thomas Zehetmair as leader of the strings has Mozart's G minor Piano Quartet as a generous extra (Philips 446 001-2). Sir Clifford Curzon's much older but pellucid version with members of the Vienna Octet has Dvořák's Piano Quintet as a no less generous offering (Decca 448 602-2).

Four

1822
SYMPHONY NO. 7 (8) IN B MINOR
('UNFINISHED'), D759

Allegro moderato   Andante con moto

There is no real mystery about why Schubert left his 'Unfinished' un-finished. Nobody stole, lost or destroyed its missing movements. No envious Salieri hid them in a drawer, even though it was in a drawer that the two completed movements were finally found more than forty years after Schubert wrote them. Nor is there much point in seeking some strange reason for Schubert's decision to abandon the work. The 'Unfinished' was not his only unfinished symphony – there are five or more – nor by any means his only unfinished work. He was a prolific and prodigal genius, quick to turn his attention from one manuscript to another, especially if he had reached a blockage in his inspiration. The year 1822, when he wrote it, was a busy one for Schubert. Posterity can count itself lucky that he completed as many masterpieces in it (among them the underrated opera *Alfonso and Estrella*, the A flat Mass and the *Wanderer Fantasy*) as he did.

Not necessarily more relevant – though in recent years more fascinating – is the American musicological theory that the harmonies of the 'Unfinished', and its unusual symphonic key of B minor, reveal Schubert to have been homosexual. Perhaps this represents no great advance on Sir George Grove's observations a century ago on the composer's supposedly 'feminine' style. Yet recently it has been hotly disputed by British authorities as well as by romantics everywhere (though especially in Austria), who believe that the young composer spent his time chasing girls.

At least the subject is providing plenty of scope for new Schubert research, such as Alex Ross's detailed examination in the *New Yorker* magazine of the poets who switched Schubert on. Whether Schubert's feelings of 'alienation', as conveyed in his music, were the outcome of a homosexual nature, or derived from illness, depression or failure to win the public acclaim he deserved, remains of course debatable. The acclaim, as we now know, was often greater than it has been made out to be.

The harmonies and modulations of the 'Unfinished', homosexual or otherwise, are undoubtedly among its most notable features, along with its strength of structure and the choice of B minor as the key of the first movement. Symphonies in Schubert's time were not (or very rarely) written in B minor, as those of Beethoven and, before him, Haydn and Mozart testify – though Tchaikovsky, significantly enough, would compose his 'Pathétique' and 'Manfred' symphonies in that key. But since Schubert considered B minor (and its B major counterpart) to possess a peculiar, perhaps private, emotional intensity – he chose it also for some of his most despairing songs – clearly his personal identification with it was strong enough to make him override symphonic tradition.

Its special colouring, at any rate, casts its shadow immediately over the sepulchral theme on the cellos and basses with which the music seems almost to rise from the grave, and over the rustling violins and wailing woodwind that sustain the mood. Not until the arrival of the famously 'consoling', though conspicuously short-lived, G major second subject on the cellos is there any hint of respite; but a sort of heroic despondency soon returns, and is extended, much more violently, into the development section, where rasping trombones, pounding kettledrums and shuddering tremoli add a demonic element to the claustrophobic gloom.

The E major andante is the first movement's obverse, transforming the symphony's two completed movements into an unintentional but perfectly balanced entity. The similarity of pace and pulse makes the second movement, indeed, seem like an extension of the first. Whether it is really possible to find what is often described as 'calm serenity' in this movement, or simply a different sort of desolation, is the type of question the 'Unfinished' symphony increasingly raises. But there is surely no doubt about the minor-key inflections, which destabilise the major-key tranquillity, nor about the fragile, transitory beauty of the long, fine-spun woodwind melody, with its ensuing, no less beautiful variant, which twice unwinds so poignantly.

Schubert composed his 'Unfinished' symphony at the age of 25, at the time when he first showed serious symptoms of what nowadays is deduced to have been syphilis. From his sketch of a scherzo, and the (unconvincing) supposition that the 'lost' finale might conceivably have been the B minor Entr'acte from *Rosamunde*, various 'finished' versions of the work have been assembled and performed. Though these naturally prove interesting to hear, the work as it stands is generally regarded as emotionally and, indeed, structurally self-sufficient. By not finishing his 'Unfinished', Schubert in a sense finished it.

Among its many recordings, there is no obvious best, but there is certainly a less obvious one – Nikolaus Harnoncourt's with the Amsterdam Concertgebouw Orchestra, which sounds more authentically Schubertian, more disturbing and sharper-edged than those of other Austrian or German conductors such as Karl Boehm, Herbert von Karajan or Gunter Wand. Though Harnoncourt's touch is light – indeed refreshingly so – the music's message is delivered at strength. This is Schubert more bitter than sweet, which is as it should be. The performance forms part of the complete medium-priced set already praised in these pages (DG 427 645-2GH), but is also available separately.

Five

1822
WANDERER FANTASY, D760

Allegro con fuoco ma non troppo – Adagio – Presto – Allegro

The *Wanderer Fantasy*, or Fantasy in C major as the composer himself called it, was one of the works – perhaps the one special work – which in some way prompted Schubert in the autumn of 1822 to leave his 'Unfinished' symphony unfinished. The reason for his decision, if there was ever a specific reason, is something we shall probably never know. His correspondence of the period makes no reference to it. But the music of this great C major Fantasy, with its quite exceptional virtuosity, suggests that it could have formed a deliberate escape route from the brooding introversion of the symphony's first two movements and the start of a scherzo which has been deemed by posterity to look unpromisingly stagnant. Perhaps it seemed so to Schubert, too. Maybe he intended to get back to the 'Unfinished' one day. At any rate, the chance to get on with something totally new and different proved at that point irresistible.

There was, moreover, a powerful incentive for writing this masterpiece for solo piano. Unlike the symphony, which had no immediate prospect of performance, the fantasy was written for 'a certain wealthy person', as Schubert described the landowner and adroit amateur pianist, Emanuel Karl Liebenberg, who had commissioned it. Unlike Beethoven, Schubert had few wealthy patrons, which must have made the invitation seem all the more attractive.

Judged simply by the work's ebullient opening bars, the commission must indeed have excited Schubert. The music hurtles along with the same sort of pulsating energy which powers the first movement of Beethoven's *Waldstein* sonata, written eighteen years earlier in the same key. Yet Schubert's fantasy is far more than an exercise in keyboard bravura, triggered though it was by a pianist endowed with a technique more spectacular than the composer's own. Schubert's hands, as he was well aware, were too small for the music's considerable demands. Though this did not deter him from playing it to friends, it once provoked him, after a mishap in the final section, to stride impatiently away from the keyboard – if a man as tiny as Schubert could ever have been said to stride – exclaiming 'Oh, let the devil play this stuff'.

But then, by the standards of Schubert's other keyboard works, this was indeed devilish music. Liszt's decision to make his own flamboyant arrangement of it for piano and orchestra thirty years later was not really surprising, and indeed helped to popularise a work which had received fewer performances than it deserved. Yet Liszt's addition of an orchestra was beside the point. The work sounded quite orchestral enough in the first place, with its evocation of string *tremoli* and other effects. As Alfred Brendel has perceptively noted, no previous composer – not even Beethoven, he might have added – had gone so far beyond the possibilities of contemporary instruments as Schubert did here.

The point about Schubert's C major Fantasy, however, is not so much its unusually hectic brilliance – the composer asked that the first movement be played with special fire – as its rigorously integrated structure. This aspect of the work, being concerned principally with the adventures of a single theme in the course of four connected movements, must have been something that appealed to Liszt, whose B minor Sonata would become another great example of structural cogency. That it could be said in many ways to anticipate Liszt's own obsession with musical metamorphosis is just one more of its startling and prophetic features.

Whether or not the fantasy's feverish impulse stems from 25-year-old Schubert's growing awareness that he was seriously ill, or merely from the fact that he was in the process of moving house, remains one of the mysteries of genius. Beneath the work's often seething activity, however, lies a carefully considered ground plan, which does not come properly into focus until the arrival of the slow second movement. Here, in a masterfully graded diminuendo, the pace of the opening allegro decelerates to adagio for a deep meditation on one of Schubert's great archetypal songs, 'Der Wanderer', written six years previously.

Only at this point does the dactylic rhythm of the fantasy's opening movement – the same rhythm which Beethoven had employed in the funereal allegretto of his Seventh Symphony and which Verdi would use for the offstage chorus in the death scene of *La Traviata* – find its explanation in the measured tread of the piano version of the song. Poetic meaning is fused into the work's structure by way of the unspoken (but already familiar) words of the song – 'There, where you are not, only there is happiness' – which inspired a heartbreakingly Schubertian expression of longing for the unattainable.

Even without the words, the music's message is made profoundly clear through the wealth of Schubertian modulation, the changes of mood and the sudden passionate eruptions of restless feeling, all achieved with a unity of effect that allows for a vigorously conventional – conventional? – scherzo and finale to provide this fantasy with the integrated outcome which Schubert had denied his listeners in the 'Unfinished' symphony. In the scherzo, a Viennese-sounding melody, already heard in the opening movement in one of Schubert's flattened keys, is brought back in scintillating waltz-time. In the finale, there is a powerful fugue, reminding us that the art of the fantasy, however romantic it became in the nineteenth century, had baroque and thoroughly Bachian roots.

Few recordings of the fantasy come to grips with all aspects of this challenging and protean work. Alfred Brendel's predictably does so, with the bigger and more introspective B flat major Sonata, D960, as coupling (Philips 420 644-2). Maurizio Pollini's impeccable performance likewise carries the stamp of a great Schubert exponent, with Schumann's C major Fantasy, written fourteen years later, continuing the vein (DG 447 451-2).

Both these established recordings have the advantage of being available now at bargain price, whereas Andras Schiff's more recent performance is rather dearer. But its precise response (on a fine and appropriate Viennese Bosendorfer piano) to every change of tempo, colour and mood is vividly graphic. Its coupling, a poetic account of Schubert's other C major Fantasy – the one for piano and violin, from towards the end of his life – proves Yuuko Shiokawa to be a frail, shadowy, sometimes quite eerie-toned champion of this fascinating, elusive work (ECM 464 320-2).

Six

1823
DIE SCHÖNE MÜLLERIN, D795

As one of today's most forthright Schubert scholars has succinctly put it: 'We know that the genesis of the [*Die schöne Müllerin*] cycle is interwoven with the beginning of the end of Schubert's life.' The composer's own suspicion that, at the age of 26, he was en route to his death five years later must surely have influenced his choice of subject. A sense of doom increasingly intrudes upon the airiness of what Schubert-lovers were once prone to describe as his 'lilting' music. In 1823, the year in which he discovered Wilhelm Müller's poetry and realised what he could do with it, Schubert was already aware that his sexual promiscuity, either with men or with the servant girls who appear to have been the alternative, had resulted in venereal disease – all the evidence points to syphilis – and that his days were therefore numbered. 'Imagine a man', he wrote in a letter, 'whose most brilliant hopes have perished, to whom the felicity of love and friendship have nothing to offer but pain at best.' With these words, he placed in perspective the yearnings so touchingly expressed in *Die schöne Müllerin*.

Though Schubert referred to the music as no more than 'a few mill-songs', there was no doubt about the seriousness with which he tackled it. Why he omitted three of the poems is a question increasingly asked, and may (or may not) be of some Schubertian significance. That the eleventh song, 'Mein!' ('Mine!'), forms the cycle's turning point is traditionally agreed – though Charles Rosen, in his book entitled *The Romantic Generation*, places it one song earlier, in 'Thränenregen' ('Shower of Tears'). This, as Rosen astutely points out, is the only song with all the verbs in the past tense, implying that it represents not an immediate experience but a memory: 'The poet and the miller's daughter were sitting at night looking at the reflections in the stream – their own reflections, the moon and the stars. The first three stanzas are set strophically, and the third opens with a premonition of suicide.'

Whatever attracted Schubert to Müller's poems, there is no doubt that this song cycle – the first of only two by him, written at a time when Beethoven's *An die Ferne geliebte* ('To the Distant Loved One') was their only real precedent – formed a major milestone in his output. Rustic maidens and miller boys being common subject matter in Schubert's day, we should perhaps remember not to dig too deeply into the meaning of these songs – yet the music consistently urges us to do so. The imagery may seem simple; but Schubert's treatment of it is nothing of the kind.

Even the poems themselves, once deemed mawkishly trivial, are today treated quite seriously. They were, after all, not unambitious. In his rhyming prologue to this tale of suicidal love, the Dessau-born poet addressed his readers as if they were an audience, promising them that what they were about to experience was 'a brand-new play' and, more than that, 'a monodrama'.

Happily for posterity, Schubert was not tempted to transform Müller's play or monodrama into an opera – though he might well have done so, with the beautiful maid of the mill as the soprano *femme fatale*, the miller lad as the tragic tenor hero, the huntsman as the brutal baritone villain, and the miller himself as the conventional father-figure of nineteenth-century *Singspiel*. He could even have added choruses of rollicking mill workers and huntsmen, and have underpinned his picturesque material (as Janáček's *Jenufa* later would do) with an orchestral part imitating the sound of a mill wheel.

But Schubert's gifts were not at their strongest in opera, even if they were not invariably as weak as they have been made out to be. Instead, he did with Müller's poems something he had never done before. With Beethoven's distant loved one as his example, he transformed them into a song cycle in which a single voice – unaided by action or props – had the responsibility of dramatising the story of the boy who loved (or imagined he loved) a miller's daughter, lost her to someone more manly, and drowned himself in the brook whose gentle murmur haunts not only the poems but the music. Though there have been foolish attempts to stage *Die schöne Müllerin*, the music itself has rejected them. As a song cycle, it is wholly self-sufficient.

Schubert did not incorporate Müller's prologue in his cycle, but must have read it and understood its implications. 'A Monodrama,' declares Müller's speaker, 'that's the term I seek' – and he proceeds to picture a scene of flowers and sunshine, of forests, fountains and, down in the valley, a silver brooklet and a roaring mill wheel. Müller, who died almost as young as Schubert himself, published his poems in Berlin in 1821, two years before Schubert got his hands on them. They were written as a *Liederspiel*, or poetic conversation piece, in which the roles were spoken by the poet's friends. In his diary, Müller had jotted: 'I can neither play nor sing, yet when I write poetry I sing and play as well. If I could produce the tunes myself, my songs would give me more pleasure than they do now. But hopefully a congenial spirit may be found who will hear the melodies in the words and give them back to me.'

His wish was granted. In due course, the Berlin composer Josef Klein set part of *Die schöne Müllerin* to music, and Müller thanked him for his efforts, saying: 'My verses lead only a half life, a life on paper, black on white . . . till music breathes the breath of life into them.' Yet Klein was not the first to see their potential. Another Berliner, Ludwig Berger, had already set them; but it was Schubert, miles away in Vienna, who immortalised them. Whether Müller ever heard Schubert's settings, or was aware of their existence, remains unknown. Certainly the music was published, in five volumes, in 1824. But that was in Vienna, not Berlin – and Müller died that year, still saying, in a letter, that he longed for a 'kindred spirit' whose ear would catch the melodies from his words.

Schubert caught the melodies, and a lot more besides. The idea of a thematic series of songs shot through with water imagery of a sort to which he responded – Brian Newbould in his study of the composer has called them 'snapshots' – fired Schubert's imagination. And, though his operas seldom disclosed signs of genius, he knew exactly how to supply operatic material into the voice, the facial expressions and the physical gestures of a single singer accompanied by a perceptive pianist (ideally Schubert himself, though in the twentieth century another composer, Benjamin Britten, regularly deputised for him in performances of uncommon perception). Books have been written about how recitalists should 'act' *Die schöne Müllerin*. The great soprano Lotte Lehmann advised would-be performers to 'lean down towards the brook and see its waters, like a luminous veil, rippling on over the image of your beloved'.

Of the poems which form *Die schöne Müllerin*, Schubert set twenty. He called them, punningly, his *Müllerlieder*, and proceeded four years later to set a further twenty-four that Müller had penned under the capacious title of *Poems from the Posthumous Papers of an Itinerant Hornist*. This second cycle, *Winterreise*, was the obverse of the first, its theme consistently bleaker in its portrayal of a desolate lover crossing a winter landscape amid snarling dogs and other alienating symbols. But though the *Müllerin* songs deal, however ironically, with springtime, and have green as their predominant colour, their message is similarly wintry. The green of the landscape, the green of the lute-ribbon and the green of the hated huntsman are reflected in the singer's changing attitudes to that colour. But the moods of the brook, too, are progressively conveyed – again via the singer's moods of the moment – in the gently rippling early songs, in the violence of 'Eifersucht und Stolz', and in the final balm of 'Des Baches Wiegenlied', where the stream intones its caressing lullaby over the drowned youth's body.

Though *Die schöne Müllerin* is often sung by a baritone, Schubert composed it for a tenor voice, which suits the music's lightness of touch without seeming too light for the cycle's tragic ending. Baritones, on the other hand, tend to darken the tone of the music much too soon, and the downward transposition of the piano part can make some of the songs – not least the very first one – sound too lumbering. Ian Bostridge's recording, dating from 1995, has all the virtues. It is youthful, passionate, plaintive, beautifully articulated and, with Graham Johnson as pianist, wholly attuned to the music's gentle but very Schubertian progress towards self-destruction. As part of Johnson's comprehensive recording of Schubert's 600-odd songs with different singers, it comes in a neat box with uncommonly detailed notes and, as an appendix, the missing poems spoken by Dietrich Fischer-Dieskau (Hyperion CDJ33025).

Yet Bostridge's, like Peter Pears's in the past, is an English tenor voice it is possible to dislike. If you have the misfortune to do so, then consider the less well-known but exemplary Werner Gura (Harmonia Mundi HMC90 1708) as a rewarding alternative, or else opt for a baritone, preferably Dietrich Fischer-Dieskau in his classic recording with Gerald Moore (EMI CDM5 66907-2).

Seven

1824
OCTET IN F MAJOR, D803

Adagio – Allegro	Adagio
Scherzo: Allegro vivace	Andante
Menuetto: Allegretto	Andante molto – Allegro

Along with the 'Trout' quintet, with which it is frequently compared, Schubert's Octet in F major has been hailed as one of the crowning masterpieces of Austrian entertainment music, sumptuously melodious, genially scored, brimming with good cheer, confirming one view – the traditional view – of Schubert as a happy purveyor of lilting dance rhythms and Viennese charm.

At a superficial level – what might be called the *Blossom Time* level – the music is indeed all these things, and can be listened to, or simply overheard, as something undistractingly enjoyable. Perhaps that was how Schubert meant it to sound; but there is more than enough evidence in its six movements to suggest that his intentions were often quite different. The point about Schubert's solitary octet is that, beneath its seemingly sunny surface, it is a deeply serious and often disturbing work, dating from a time of emotional crisis in its composer's life – just like so many other Schubert masterpieces, in fact.

Like Hugo Wolf and Gustav Mahler later in the nineteenth century, Schubert wrote Viennese music in which sweetness and bitterness, drama and poignancy, contentment and neurosis, fury and despair co-existed with each other. He would have been – as Mahler actually was – a good subject for Freudian analysis. He was often, or so it now seems, in one or the other extreme of manic depression, and he was certainly (like Wolf) doomed from an early age to suffer the appalling after-effects of venereal disease.

So when, in 1824, he was commissioned by Count Ferdinand Troyer, chief steward at the court of Archduke Rudolph (Beethoven's distinguished musical friend and patron), to compose an octet for wind and strings as a companion piece for Beethoven's highly popular Septet, his state of mind seemed bound to have a bearing on what he produced. He was not, after all, a man whose music contradicted his feelings at the time of writing it, or existed, as Mozart's or Beethoven's was capable of doing, on an entirely separate plane. Not until we understand this can we wholly grasp what his music is telling us about himself – and the Octet in F is no exception.

The year in which he wrote it was one in which he was increasingly ill and depressed. 'Each night when I go to sleep,' he wrote to a friend, 'I hope I will not wake again, and each morning reminds me only of yesterday's unhappiness.' Though famed for conviviality, Schubert wrote his Octet during a period of solitude. Moreover, while working on it, he fasted for a fortnight. Yet, though something of this should be audible to anyone with ears to hear what Schubert is really saying, the Octet seems from the start to have provided what a leading British biographer has described as 'unalloyed delight'.

Count Troyer, who as solo clarinettist played alongside Beethoven's friend Ignaz Schuppanzigh (leader of the great Razumovsky Quartet after which three of Beethoven's works were named) in the first performance, found himself to be the recipient of a clarinet part of conspicuous beauty and emotion. Here was music which bridged the gap between Mozart's clarinet masterpieces for his friend Anton Stadler and Brahms's for the similarly gifted Richard Mühlfeld. The terms of the commission were wholly fulfilled, and Schubert's Octet has served, right up to the present, as a regular companion piece for Beethoven's Septet, written for the same combination of instruments minus one violin. This was not just another piece of Schubertian 'house music', however inspired, but a work clearly designed for performance by some of the leading Viennese musicians of the day.

Nor did it need Beethoven as chaperon, as anyone can now hear. Indeed, it is all the better without the support of the work which, structurally, Schubert employed as his model, to the extent that he wrote the same number of movements in much the same running order and with the same instrumental timbres. Yet its personality is entirely different, even though, when played side by side, the similarities between the two works are what tend to be noticed. For this reason, they are best kept apart if the Schubert – traditionally performed directly after the Beethoven – is to be heard to proper advantage.

Thus the slow, groping introduction to Schubert's first movement sounds all the more effective when it emerges from nowhere, and its dotted rhythms (a feature of the entire work) sound all the starker. Some of the introductory material reappears in more genial form in the ensuing allegro, which is launched with a typically Schubertian upsurge of energy, and with a terse opening theme whose leaping rhythm clearly derives from the slow introduction. A second important theme, voiced first by the clarinet and then taken up by the horn, also harks back to the embryonic introduction and later brings the movement calmly to its close.

The slow second movement could be a thanksgiving to Troyer for commissioning the work, for it starts with a long, lyrical clarinet solo over an arpeggiated accompaniment which anticipates Schubert's famous setting of *Ave Maria*, composed the following year. The atmosphere seems placidly pastoral, but it is shattered towards the end by one of those dark Schubertian intimations of mortality which increasingly thrust their way into his music, and which were similarly to invade the works of his successor Gustav Mahler.

Surprisingly, even some of Schubert's most perceptive champions have failed to identify the death-laden atmosphere which pervades this movement even at its most seemingly serene. Yet how else are we to interpret its unsettling changes of key, or the plaintive descant played by the clarinet at the point where the first violin takes over the theme, or, above all, the sudden descent and stoppage of this ethereal melody in mid-air in the course of the movement's closing pages? It is almost as if, in today's parlance, an aircraft flying through placid skies has suffered a catastrophic accident. The stabbing pizzicato note from the cello and bass at this point tells its own story. Thereafter the clarinet tries poignantly to resume the melody, but the harmony keeps going wrong – the calm of the opening of the movement has been irretrievably lost. Yet a commentator of Alfred Einstein's eminence could find 'no trace of duality' in this work.

The succeeding scherzo reassuringly restores equilibrium with a fast, bouncing main theme (delightfully extended at one point by the clarinet) and a quietly Viennese middle section played by the violins over a humorous bass. The fourth movement, ostensibly light-hearted, is a set of seven variations on an ambling theme from Schubert's opera, *Die Freunde von Salamanka*, a rarity which has been featured in the Edinburgh Festival. The treatment recalls the variations in the 'Trout' quintet, and the movement culminates in a hilarious, breakneck variation with a prominent part for the first violin, followed by a final lingering statement of the theme.

Yet, just before this violin variation, there has been another of Schubert's moments of crisis, when the key (bright C major at the start of the movement) moves into A flat, and the music gains a sudden edge of melancholy intensity. Nor does the succeeding minuet, for all its simplicity, banish the mood. On the surface, everything is dreamily Viennese, but again the undercurrents are there, particularly in the music's tendency towards flattened keys – a regular Schubert fingerprint, it's true, but one that here carries no hint of ordinariness. After the central trio section, with its charming triplet figure, and after the reprise of the minuet, Schubert unexpectedly adds a nineteen-bar coda, begun by the horn, characteristically ambiguous in mood and tonality.

The sense of mystery is maintained, not to say increased, in the slow introduction to the finale, with its tense *tremolandi* and its rapid lurches between loud and soft tone. The main body of the movement, with its springy, quick-marching main theme, is more jovial, but towards the end the *tremolandi* return like spectres at the feast. They are, however, finally thrust aside by a whizzing Allegro molto coda. Life for the moment has conquered death, though Schubert at the age of 27 was already in its shadow.

Though it is possible to have a conductor for Schubert's Octet, as a French ensemble once confirmed at the Edinburgh Festival, the results are likely to be unrewarding. Rapport between the players is paramount, and, so long as they are good enough and can grasp the music's implications, all is likely to be well. The best recordings likewise tend to come from performers accustomed to playing chamber music together and capable of retaining the intimate atmosphere of the music. Slickness, in Schubert's Octet, is something to be shunned. Among innumerable versions of the long work, the Vienna Octet's continues to stand out. The players, while obviously Viennese virtuosi, never sound out of touch with the music's inner nature, and convey each movement with translucent beauty and feeling (Decca 448 715-2DEC). No less enthralling, and perhaps even more responsive to the music's emotional implications, is a recording on period instruments by members of the Academy of Ancient Music, an ensemble far less dry than its name may suggest (L'Oiseau-Lyre 425 519-2).

Eight

1824
STRING QUARTET IN A MINOR, D804

Allegro ma non troppo

Menuetto: Allegretto

Andante

Allegro moderato

Schubert was only 27 – or, to put it another way, just four years short of his death – when he composed his A minor and D minor ('Death and the Maiden') string quartets. But whichever angle you approach them from, they are masterpieces of the first rank and music of his full maturity. Though Sir Donald Tovey, Edinburgh's distinguished analytical essayist, delivered a famous – today we might prefer to call it notorious – dictum about all Schubert's works being 'early' works, there is no doubt that once the composer was into his twenties his inspiration speedily outstripped his years. His first quartets, more than a dozen of them, had been written for domestic performance by members of the Schubert family circle, with the composer himself as viola-player. For that reason, they are traditionally dismissed as prentice pieces. Yet there is no doubt that by the time of the

A minor Quartet his music was steadily deepening and, more often than not, darkening. The gregarious composer who, according to popular belief, had been the soul of conviviality was suddenly capable of locking himself indoors and refusing to talk to friends.

Various theories have been voiced about the reason for this apparent personality change. Perhaps, as has been increasingly suspected, there was in Schubert an element of manic depression. Perhaps, as modern medical opinion has proposed, venereal disease was the root cause of the physical and emotional problems of the last years of his short life, bringing with it the awareness that he would soon die. Certainly the poignancy of the A minor Quartet – the quiet yet anguished obverse of the more dynamic and dramatic 'Death and the Maiden' – is one of the most moving expressions of Schubert's growing introspection around that time, though astute listeners have claimed to trace it back much further.

But Schubert's life was changing in other ways, too. Schoolteaching having ceased to satisfy him, he gave it up. Unlike Haydn before him, he had never been a court composer with his own orchestra and opera company to practise on – though he did rely on neighbourhood orchestras and circles of friends as testing grounds for his music. Unlike Mozart and Beethoven, he was not a good enough pianist to establish himself publicly as a virtuoso performer of his own works. And he was too reticent to attract influential patrons.

What he did have, in his modest way, was high ambition – and the A minor Quartet, originally numbered Op. 29, No. 1, was his first major announcement of it. He was confident enough to promote it as a public piece rather than confine it to people's houses. Ignaz Schuppanzigh's great Viennese string quartet, having already championed Beethoven, agreed to feature it in a subscription concert at the Gesellschaft der Musikfreunde in March 1824. The performance, favourably reviewed in the Leipzig *Allgemeine Musikalische Zeitung*, was an event. Schubert had reached a milestone in his life, and 'Death and the Maiden', his next quartet, took him beyond it.

Both these works gain a special eloquence through being song-obsessed, not simply in the sense that they contain songlike melodies but in the way they make use of genuine Schubert songs, thereby enabling listeners to find connections between music and words. The D minor Quartet is inevitably coloured by the presence of the song, 'Death and the Maiden', upon which Schubert based the variations that form the slow movement. The A minor Quartet is similarly associated with the B flat major entr'acte from the *Rosamunde* incidental music – not quite a song, though it could easily have become one. Again the melody is employed as the basis of a set of variations, wistful to start with but passionately developing as the movement progresses.

Yet the work's songlike bitter-sweetness has been present from the start of the first movement, with its long, tender theme opening with the same three notes that would later launch Verdi's Requiem so hauntingly. It is sung by the first violin over a winding, throbbing accompaniment reminiscent of Schubert's plaintive setting of 'Gretchen am Spinnrade', composed ten years earlier. As one biographer has pointed out, the Goethe poem which inspired Schubert's song was much on his mind at the time. It seems hardly a coincidence that, just before writing the quartet, he had declared: 'My peace is gone, my heart is sore, I shall find it never and never more' – Goethe's very words.

Poetry likewise haunts the brooding third movement – a minuet only in name, whose opening phrases recall Schubert's setting of Schiller's 'Die Götter Griechenlands' ('The Greek Gods'), with its appropriate question: 'Fair world, where are you?' The melancholy drag of the cello line demolishes any Viennese charm the music might otherwise be thought to possess. Even in the gentle middle section, the music's effect is curiously despairing, as if Schubert is ruefully recalling happier times he knows will never return.

Only in the finale, a sturdily dancing movement with a mock Hungarian accent, is the pathos at least partly expelled. Or is it? Here, too, there is surely an extraordinary sadness behind the nimble grace-notes and the little lingerings of the main theme. The cheerfulness, if the music can be called cheerful at all, is only skin-deep. If this is Schubert's evocation of a ballroom, as some people have claimed, it is a room filled with spectres.

The fragility of this music is conveyed by the Quatuor Mosaïques in a 1995 recording which employs original instruments to ethereal effect. In the hands of these heartfelt players, it is not just the finale but the entire work whose sound speaks of spectres. But though the notes may seem blanched, the emotion is there – and all the more disturbing because it is so trancelike.

Nor is the early E flat major Quartet, D87, which completes the disc, merely a makeweight. A teenage work written for the Schubert family to play, it was dismissed by the Schubert and Mozart expert, Alfred Einstein, as 'Mozart from beginning to end'. On the contrary, it is pure Schubert, so much so that it was thought for years to be one of his late works, which was why a misleading opus number, Op. 125, No. 1, was applied to it. If that had been correct, its sunniness would have seemed like a gleam of light amid the desolation of Schubert's last years. E flat major is a warm key. His decision to write all four movements in it may have limited the colour contrasts available to him; but the result of this self-imposed discipline is wonderfully unified, as the Quatuor Mosaïques have no difficulty confirming (Auvidis Astree E8580).

NOTES ON SCHUBERT

The first thing to be said about Schubert's piano sonatas — and the great Schubert pianist Artur Schnabel was reputedly the first to say it — is that they are dramatic works. Yet that is not the word most widely applied to them. Lyrical, melodious, smiling, bubbling, songlike, bitter-sweet — all the standard Schubert adjectives — are what they are accepted as being, with 'prolix' and 'clumsy' as more hostile epithets. But whatever one chooses to call them (and clumsiness, like prolixity, in Schubert is the fault of the performer), it has taken people a long time to recognise the importance of the sonatas as an entity. But today, at last, they hold the position they deserve in Schubert's output. Until you know them, you cannot claim to know Schubert — which was hardly what was said about them fifty years ago.

Of the twenty-one numbered works, at least half were written between 1815 and 1819, but are no more to be dismissed as juvenilia than the song 'Gretchen am Spinnrade', written even earlier. Then came a pause, not broken until 1823 by the dark and disturbing A minor Sonata, D784. The next sonata is one of Schubert's C major masterpieces, undiminished by being left unfinished, or being foolishly nicknamed 'Reliquie' ('Relic'). There was, in any case, more to come, with a trilogy of sonatas in 1825–6 and a further trilogy in 1828, exploring an extraordinary range of moods, not all of them death-conscious.

Nine

1825
PIANO SONATA IN D MAJOR, D850

Allegro   Andante con moto

Scherzo: Allegro vivace   Rondo: Allegro moderato

Not until that impeccable Schubertian, Sir Clifford Curzon, played and
recorded the great D major Sonata was it recognised in Britain as the far-
flung masterpiece it is. Before that – and, sadly, sometimes afterwards –
its consistency of inspiration has been called in question. Philip Radcliffe,
in his academically pernickety BBC guidebook to these works, claimed it
to be 'on a decidedly lower level' than the sonata which preceded it. Yet
this surely is one of the glories of Viennese piano music after Beethoven,
its size and splendour in keeping with that of the 'Great' C major Symphony,
on which the composer was also at work in the year 1825. Picking holes in
Schubert continues to be a thriving industry, no matter how much better
in general his music has come to be understood.

The D major sonata, it is true, has an opening so physically action-packed – pummelling rhythms, whirling triplets – that it would be easy to accuse the first movement of possessing a lack of breathing space. Where are the pauses that so often add their own silent eloquence to Schubert's music? Yet the hectic passion, the heroic outbursts, the constant swerves from one idea to another, the hurtling energy and what Alfred Brendel has called the 'downright unrestrained *joie de vivre*' of the music carry all before them. In this particular first movement, Schubert has no time to pause.

Coming directly after the sombre tragedy of the A minor Sonata, D845, whose finale, again according to Alfred Brendel, 'crushes you into the ground', the sunlit vitality of the D major is all the more startling. The depressive side of Schubert, it would seem, has become its manic obverse. The work, centrepiece of a trilogy which ends in the epic radiance of the G major Sonata, D894, dates from what appears to have been one of Schubert's idyllic summer jaunts among the mountains and valleys of Upper Austria with his singer friend, the baritone Johann Vogl. Here and there, they gave recitals together. Schubert, aware of the musical rapport between them, reported that 'the way in which at such moments we seem to become one is something quite new and unprecedented to the people here'.

The music's almost consistent sense of bonhomie, surprising at that point in his life, evokes the delights of the 'Trout' quintet, inspired by the same pastoral surroundings six years earlier. The sound is noticeably more sophisticated, as it was bound to be; but the expected shadows, the

Schubertian moments of recognition that happiness does not last, are equally noticeably absent. The 'garden several miles in extent', the 'avenues of enormous trees to walk in for hours', the 'ranges of the highest mountains as far as the eye can see', to which Schubert referred in a letter to his brother in September 1825, may have some bearing on the sheer scale of this sonata, though not perhaps on its volatility.

Even the slow movement proves more restless than its opening theme would suggest. Though some commentators claim this to have been inspired by the start of the larghetto from Beethoven's Second Symphony, the melody, and the manner in which it is meant to be played, is so utterly and yearningly Schubertian that the resemblance seems irrelevant. The music is a species of slow-moving rondo, the melody recurring several times, on each occasion with magical alterations. The textures are rich, the rhythms elaborate, the underlying pulse powerful enough to sustain what is the longest movement of the four.

But even the succeeding scherzo is built on a substantial scale, its interplay of melodies (including a delicious example of Schubertian café music) allowed to swing without hustle from one mood to another. The central trio section relaxes enough to sound like a reminiscence of the slow movement, then the scherzo pounds off again with the grandly jerky theme with which it opened.

Nor is the finale – a further rondo – in any way hurried. To overpress the jaunty opening theme, with its tick-tock accompaniment, would be to inflict serious damage on music so dependent on perfect articulation and subtlety of rhythm. Yet its effect never lapses into daintiness. There is energy here, just as in the preceding movements, and there are sudden diversions, with backward glances at Haydn and little pastoral foretastes of Mahler. The ending, in which the movement winds down like a music box, is one of the loveliest moments in the entire work.

Alfred Brendel's deep appreciation of every facet of this work shines through his 1987 recording, which also includes a more shadowy work, the A minor Sonata, D784, as postlude (Philips 422 063-2). Mitsuko Uchida, in the same two works, is scarcely less penetrating (Philips 464 480-2); and the glorious old Curzon performance, sounding as spontaneous as ever, can be found on Decca (443 570-2) along with the six *Moments Musicaux*.

Ten

1825–6
SYMPHONY NO. 8 (9) IN C MAJOR ('GREAT'), D944

Andante – Allegro ma non troppo   Andante con moto

Scherzo: Allegro vivace   Allegro vivace

There was a time when Schubert's 'Great' C major Symphony, as we have come to call it, was thought to be unplayable. Performers were daunted not merely by what Schumann described as its 'heavenly lengths' but also by the energy needed to keep the music airborne, and by the effort required to recognise that a work so seemingly unwieldy in scale actually possessed a logical structure.

Yet the old story that the orchestra of the Vienna Gesellschaft der Musikfreunde rejected this symphony because of its size and difficulty must be taken with a pinch of salt. Much has been done recently to clean up the myths surrounding the 'Great' C major, which is now known to have been composed not in the last year of Schubert's short life but up to three years earlier. Nor, it seems, did it remain wholly unperformed until Schumann discovered it in a pile of manuscripts and passed it on to Mendelssohn to conduct in Leipzig a decade after Schubert's death. That the work was publicly rehearsed by the Gesellschaft, 'in the practices at the Conservatoire', soon after Schubert composed it has been satisfactorily verified; and the finale was publicly played in Vienna in 1836, three years before Mendelssohn unveiled the (not quite) complete work in Germany.

Yet Mendelssohn's championing of the symphony is not to be gainsaid, even if he prudently abbreviated it, as Karl Rankl was still doing with the Scottish National Orchestra as recently as the 1950s. When Mendelssohn took the work to London in 1844, the orchestral players, faced with the equestrian string figuration in the finale, shamefully laughed him off the platform, delaying the work's British premiere for another twelve years (when it was damagingly split across two evenings). Other orchestras proved equally scornful. Hornists – whose instruments, in this work, are the immediate recipients of one of Schubert's greatest themes – dismissed the symphony as tuneless. Nor were critics invariably more perceptive. Bernard Shaw, while admitting its manifold charms, reckoned it an 'exasperatingly brainless' composition.

By equating charm with brainlessness, Shaw was not alone in demeaning Schubert's mastery of symphonic form. As Tovey dryly put it: 'The truest lover of Schubert confesses that he would not wish the "Unfinished" symphony to have a typical Schubert finale.' Yet the finale of the 'Great' C major is not only masterly but also Schubertian through and through.

The entire work, indeed, displays a discernibly progressive approach to symphonic form. The first movement's slow introduction is no introduction in the normal sense but structurally integrated with the succeeding Allegro ma non troppo, not least in the meticulous matching of the tempo of the one to the tempo of the other (conductors who impose a false accelerando on the end of the introduction do Schubert no favours). The opening horn theme, steadily unfurled at a typically Schubertian walking speed, is spacious enough to fill the whole introduction, just as the scherzo's central trio section consists of a vast single melody, gloriously unfurled.

The flow of the symphony is maintained in a variety of ways. Out of the first movement's introduction, for instance, there bursts at the start of the allegro an emphatically rhythmic, jerky theme, pummelling rather than songlike, followed by a Schubertian swerve from major to minor for a quieter, more lyrical second subject on the woodwind. The momentum is never disrupted. The grand design of the music is always clear. The use of pianissimo trombones is a famous example of Schubert's flair for instrumental colouring. From time to time, the music explodes with vitality, nowhere more so than in the coda, in quicker tempo, which brings back the opening horn theme in exhilaratingly high relief – though bits and pieces of it have, in fact, formed the foundations of the whole movement. There is no excuse for broadening the tempo when the opening theme makes its final experience. Conductors who commit this popular vulgarism are thinking only of themselves, not of Schubert, who never wanted it.

The Andante con moto anticipates the melancholy walking pulse of the opening song of the *Winterreise* cycle. To start with, the music sounds calm, unhurried and, in spite of a wistful oboe tune, not too sad. But abrupt trombone chords prevent it from ever becoming placid, and the whole fabric of the movement is later torn apart by the unexpectedly violent ferocity of its climax – one of the most powerful examples of what has been recently called Schubert's 'volcanic temper', and certainly not an aspect of the composer traditionally regarded as typical. After a stunned silence and some hesitant pizzicati, consolation comes from the cellos, and the melodious flow then resumes. But the music thereafter never quite stabilises, and the ending is mournful and capricious, a mixture of louds and softs.

Nor do things grow more secure in the scherzo, which is ostensibly a Viennese dance on a grand scale, relentless in its spinning energy and stamping rhythms, shot through with wisps of melody that keep getting thrust aside by the restless motion. The trio section, though calmer in mood, sustains the momentum. So does the finale, which gallops along like a ride to the abyss. Not even the serene woodwind theme that forms the second subject – replacing what Tovey deemed to be an unpromising fugue, visibly stroked out in the composer's manuscript – provides respite, because the strings keep the rhythm constantly on the boil. A stupendous coda, filled with what sound like heavy anvil strokes, brings the symphony to a fitting close.

One of the tests of a true Schubert conductor lies in how he handles the coda of the first movement. If he suddenly steps on the brakes for the final return of the opening theme, thereby creating an air of fake grandeur, and reduces speed still further for the closing kettledrum crashes, he has undoubtedly failed. If he stays in tempo, sustaining the music's hurtling momentum, he has passed.

By this token, most performances and most recordings fail, though they can be redeemed by other factors. Mellowness, however, is a no-no, even if Bruno Walter used to make it seem an essential ingredient. The 'Great' C major Symphony is not mellow music but a hard-driven masterpiece, beautiful certainly – almost all Schubert is beautiful – but ferocious in its energy. Nikolaus Harnoncourt's recording with the Amsterdam Concertgebouw Orchestra rigorously realises the music's sweep and incisiveness, without falling back on tricks with the tempo. If you can afford a complete set of Schubert's symphonies, this is the one to buy (Teldec 4509-91184-2).

Sir Charles Mackerras's no-nonsense performance with the Scottish Chamber Orchestra, with the 'Unfinished' as a generous coupling, is also recommended, not least because the use of a smaller orchestra gives the music a lightness of touch missing from many other recordings (Telarc CD 80502).

Eleven

1826
STRING QUARTET IN D MINOR ('DEATH AND THE MAIDEN'), D810

Allegro   Andante con moto

Scherzo: Allegro molto   Presto

To call Schubert's music 'songlike' is a statement of the obvious. But, like many such statements about him, it is only half-true. As the composer of more than 600 songs, of operas, choruses, part-songs and church music, he clearly thought in terms of the human voice. Yet long stretches of his 'Great' C major Symphony have nothing to do with song, their primary concern being rhythm and impetus. The same can be said for other orchestral works – the fierce development section of the first movement of the 'Unfinished', the dynamism of some of the earlier symphonies, the pummelled-out chords in the last of his A major piano sonatas, and the opening section of the *Wanderer Fantasy* all come to mind. In many cases, it is the juxtaposition of song and non-song, encountered to powerful effect in the memorable slow movement of that same A major Sonata, which makes Schubert's works what they are.

It certainly contributes to the restlessness of the D minor Quartet. On the one hand, there is Schubert's song, 'Der Tod und das Mädchen' ('Death and the Maiden'), which, in the guise of a theme and variations, forms the heart of the work. On the other, there is the unease of the rest of the work, whose tension and pathos are maintained from start to finish. Though one Schubert authority, Arthur Hutchings, has warned against reading too deep a meaning into Schubert's choice of song for this work's central inspiration, it is hard to do otherwise. From the impatient rasp of the opening right through to the relentless tarantella that forms the finale, this is music about mortality.

Schubert set Matthias Claudius's poem into song when he was 20. The quartet followed some years later, with the song melody serving as inspiration for a series of five variations. With no immediate prospect of a performance, Schubert evidently cast the music aside but fortunately returned to it the following winter. By January 1826, the work was being rehearsed in Vienna by a group of Schubert's friends, one of whom later reported that the composer 'corrected' the freshly written instrumental parts during rehearsals. He also, it seems, made a number of cuts to lighten the load of the performers. Luckily for posterity, he did not excise these passages permanently from the score.

The premiere in February 1826 took place at the home of the operatic tenor, Joseph Barth, to whom Schubert had earlier dedicated a set of part-songs. A further performance was given later that month at the house of Franz Lechner, one of Schubert's closest friends – and one who was later to claim, fictitiously, that Schubert had thrust the quartet into a drawer and forgotten about it (though it is perfectly true that it remained in manuscript until Czerny published it in 1831, three years after Schubert's death). The first public performance took place in 1832. The unreliable Lechner, a Bavarian who had settled in Vienna, was also responsible for the theory that the opening theme of the first movement was inspired by the sound of a coffee-mill, an idea perhaps no more preposterous than the numerous other legends that have been built around this work.

What is musically more important, however, is that the harsh dry rattle of the opening chords introduces the triplet rhythm which is one of the motivating forces of the entire work, and which hurtles through the finale. Even in the first movement, these triplets are seldom out of the picture. Apart from generating most of the force of the main theme, they also serve to accompany the more gentle second subject, which is played (in contrasted rhythm) by the two violins.

In the closing bars of the first movement, the triplets make the darkest of their appearances, dying away to a staccato mutter on the cello. Most performers incorporate a massive reduction of speed – almost to the pace of a funeral march – at this point, even though the score merely says

'Tempo I'. The effect, if inauthentic, is undeniably impressive, and paves the way appropriately for the funereal tread of the slow movement, which opens with a G minor statement of the 'Death and the Maiden' melody.

In the song, the girl expresses her horror at the approach of Death – to which Death gives a consoling reply. In the quartet, the theme inspires a set of variations which never travel far from their source but which colour and decorate the theme very eloquently. The first variation principally features the first violin, and the second variation the cello. The hammering rhythms of the third variation bring powerful motion to the music, to which the soft fourth variation (with the melody on second violin and viola) provides delicate major-key contrast. The fifth variation, after a passionate opening section, gradually restores the mood of the original song.

The scherzo has a robust, swinging main theme, prophetic of the anvils that would ring in Wagner's *Rheingold* thirty years later; the central trio section, in comparison, is tender and songlike. The finale, at one time, was likened to a Dance of Death. Though this could seem too Lisztian a description, the ferocious impulse, the sudden contrasts of tone and the almost manic increase in tempo towards the end all suggest that such romantic nineteenth-century notions about the music were not so far off the mark. At any rate, after a first, second and third movement such as this quartet possesses, Schubert's swerving tarantella seems the only possible conclusion.

Gustav Mahler's increasingly popular transcription of this work for string orchestra – like the Leonard Bernstein version of Beethoven's Op. 131 quartet – is a piece of tampering which does Schubert no service. Its thickened textures, and undertow of double-bass tone, dull the edge of the music. Its current revival is an act of opportunism on the part of concert-promoters which can only be deplored.

Being the antithesis of the A minor Quartet, the D minor calls for a more forthright, less reflective sort of performance. Yet an assertive account of the A minor can be made to work, as America's Emerson Quartet has proved in a challenging recording; and the same may be true of a spectral account of the D minor. Most recordings of it, however, are far from spectral, except at the start of the slow movement. The New Leipzig Quartet's performance has a contained power that is altogether masterly, and the disc – part of a fascinating complete set, but available separately – is eked out with a bundle of atmospheric Schubert minuets and other dances from his early domestic period (MDG 307 0604-2).

The Quartetto Italiano's fine recording from the 1960s is also recommended, not least because this bargain-price two-disc set contains all three of Schubert's last quartets plus the passionate fragment of his unfinished C minor Quartet (Philips 446 163-2). As a slice of Schubert history, however, the Busch Quartet's 1936 performances of the D minor and A minor quartets remain unsurpassed for their vibrancy and eloquence, every line carved with clarity (EMI CDH7 69795-2, another bargain).

Twelve

1826
STRING QUARTET IN G MAJOR, D887

Allegro molto moderato

Andante un poco moto

Scherzo: Allegro vivace

Allegro assai

Among the many sharp *aperçus* in the posthumously published diaries of the drama critic Kenneth Tynan is an unexpected comment on Schubert. Reflecting on the adagio from an unidentified piece of chamber music, he asserts that 'there is nothing more beautiful than the happy moments of unhappy men'. This, he adds, 'might serve as a definition of art'.

Bearing in mind that Schubert's chamber music contains very few adagios – he much preferred the walking pace of andantes – it seems likely that Tynan had been listening either to the great C major String Quintet, whose adagio is not happy at all, or to the F major Octet, where the adagio is all the more disturbing because, beneath its seemingly serene surface, its consciousness of mortality is conveyed by such destabilising harmonies.

But finding happiness in Schubert where none exists is a traditional misconception – just as traditional as claiming Schubert himself to have been a cheerful little man, much given to playing the piano at parties. Tynan, at least, did not pursue this false trail. The point he made was perfectly sound, even if he chose the wrong work with which to illustrate it.

In Schubert's chamber music, indeed, there is very little happiness – and, in his three last and greatest string quartets, with the 'Great' C major Symphony and the *Winterreise* song cycle looming in the background, there is nothing but an acute awareness of life's transience. The first of these quartets – the A minor, formerly known as Op. 29 – may be 'lyrical' (a portmanteau word much applied to Schubert), perhaps even wistful, though 'dreamlike sadness' might be a better description of the veiled and melancholy sweetness that permeates it. The next work, assembled around the song 'Death and the Maiden', speaks for itself. But not even this demonic masterpiece prepares us for the ferocious assault of the G major Quartet (Op. 161 as once was), a work often described, though not in praise, as 'orchestral' in its sound effects, but which gains its startling intensity of expression from the very fact that it is actually a string quartet.

The belief that Schubert took just ten days to write it in 1826 presents yet another of the misleading pictures that have existed of him – that of the 'instinctive' composer who never needed to work things out or rethink what he had jotted down. To what extent he wrestled with the G major

Quartet, or how many drafts he made of it, are things we are unlikely ever to know, because the evidence has never been found. But a glance at the opening page does not suggest something that sprang at speed into Schubert's mind. What that page does suggest, as does the opening of the C major String Quintet, is his ability to hint at the long-term harmonic structure of a piece in a very few bars. If the quintet, as we shall see, is a vast attack on the security of its home key of C major (which remains under threat even in the closing bars of the finale nearly an hour later), so the quartet is a premeditated attack on G major, which in the very opening chord dissolves instantly and alarmingly into G minor. The effect is almost palpable, and in one form or another it will recur again and again – and all the more potently when, in the first movement's recapitulation, it suddenly reverses from G minor to G major.

If, as has been claimed, the jerky dotted rhythms and tremolos of the first movement are prophetic of Schubert's compatriot, Anton Bruckner, their intensity and violence belong to a quite different world. When he composed this work at the age of 29, thoughts of death were nothing new to him. Already chronically ill, he had written of how 'each morning only recalls the miseries of the day before'. Not for nothing, in our own time, did Woody Allen employ this quartet on the soundtrack of one of his most sombre films, underpinning the action to powerful emotional effect.

When, eventually, the first movement has run its course – and, if the exposition repeat is included, this will have taken more than twenty minutes

– the slow movement in E minor trudges into the world of *Winterreise*, which Schubert did not compose until shortly before his death two years later. But it is already there in the poignant, elegiac stride of the cello theme, and in the anguish of the two despairing outbursts that bring the music almost to breaking point. In these (the first of them significantly in G minor), the tremolos of the first movement gain a fresh violence, while violin scales flare like explosions of what has been called Schubert's 'volcanic' temper.

The feverishly mercurial scherzo relaxes only during its central trio section, a hauntingly graceful Austrian waltz of a sort which one distinguished Schubert authority, Sir Jack Westrup, must have felt tempted to dismiss as Viennese café music (a description he reserved for the magnificent finale of the C major Quintet). The fast and lurching finale – a sort of tenebrous tarantella – brings back the full force of the first movement's major–minor tensions, in which, as another Schubert authority, John Reed, has pertinently put it, G major *is* G minor. True, he goes on to declare – in the manner of so many other backstabbing Schubert experts – that it sums up the work's argument 'without adding very much to it'. As the grimmest of Schubert's rides to the abyss, however, it could hardly be bettered or, in its sardonic relentlessness, seem more obsessively appropriate.

Being by far the most tiring of Schubert's quartets to perform, the G major features less frequently than the A minor and D minor quartets in concert programmes – it was for that reason, as a member of the Amadeus Quartet confessed in an interview with the present writer, that performers tend to avoid taking it on tour with them. Yet a sense of strain should be an element of every performance of this work. To make it sound easy, to give it what is all too readily described as Schubertian 'fluency', is to miss its point.

Neither the Manchester-based Lindsay Quartet, in their typically tense and perceptive recording, nor the less familiar (in Britain at least) New Leipzig Quartet commits this error. For those who love the Lindsays, their performance is the obvious choice (ASV CDDCA661). But the Leipzigers, too, provide a special experience. Facing the challenge of what sounds like a dry acoustic, they bring a starkness to the music which is utterly arresting yet never overrides its moments of sweetness. The disc (MDG 307 0601-2) forms part of a complete set employing the Urtext of the New Schubert Edition, but can be bought separately. It includes, as a bonus, fragments of two unfinished works.

Thirteen

1827
FOUR IMPROMPTUS, D899

No. 1 in C minor

No. 2 in E flat major

No. 3 in G flat major

No. 4 in A flat major

FOUR IMPROMPTUS, D935

No. 1 in F minor

No. 2 in A flat major

No. 3 in B flat major

No. 4 in F minor

Though Schubert's piano sonatas are now recognised as vital large-scale components of his output, they were once considered so inferior to Beethoven's that they did not merit serious attention. His sets of shorter piano pieces, on the other hand, were overshadowed by nobody else's. Moreover, being easier to grasp and less tiring to perform, they had no difficulty establishing themselves as little miracles of musical characterisation. The fact that the two sets of impromptus, D899 and D935, were once thought to be sonatas in disguise did nothing to diminish their popularity or to stop pianists from splitting them up as separate *morceaux*. Written late in the penultimate year of his life, and shortly before he embarked on his last three great and genuine piano sonatas, they nevertheless benefit from being treated as entities.

What's in a name? 'Impromptu' implies something improvised; but Robert Schumann, that passionate musical cryptographer, was one of the first to propose that Schubert was here deliberately concealing something more ambitious. His evidence was based on the second set, with its abundance of sonata-like features and its return in the end to the key in which it begins. But the first set, which begins in one key and ends in another, seems unified principally by the fact that the four pieces are all by Schubert. In no sense do they form an integer; yet, in an uncanny way, that is how they sound.

The term 'impromptu' was in any case a bit vague in 1827. Vořišek, the conductor of Vienna's Gesellschaft der Musikfreunde and thus known to Schubert, had pioneered it with an impromptu written five years earlier. If Schubert's pieces do in some ways sound improvisatory, this is merely the impression given by them. Quite clearly, they were meticulously composed.

Of the four that form D899 (originally grouped as Opus 90), the first is inspired almost entirely by a melancholy little march tune, its notes picked out skeletally and haltingly before being harmonised. The second is a brilliant, fiery example of what Chopin might have called an *étude*, setting right-hand triplets against a left-hand rhythmic pattern (Brahms, in a resourceful arrangement of it, put the triplets in the left hand). The third is a serenely flowing idyll – sweet, sad, sublime – based on one of the most gently rippling and unforgettable of all Schubert melodies. In the fourth, there are flashing arpeggios surrounding a ruggedly Beethovenian middle section.

Schubert was dead before Schumann identified, to his own satisfaction, the second set of impromptus, D935, as a sonata in disguise, with F minor as its home key. Whatever Schubert himself had thought about them, he was pragmatic enough to tell his publisher that the pieces, formerly known as Op. 142, could be performed separately or together, and he numbered them 5–8 as proof that they formed a continuation of the earlier set.

Sonata or otherwise – and all Schubert authorities today opt for otherwise – the music does have its own unity, the pieces offsetting each other to perfection. Yet each, as the composer clearly recognised, seems thoroughly self-sufficient, in a way that a sonata movement usually does not – though perhaps we should ask ourselves if Schubert's choice of title has any bearing on how we listen to the music.

But if Schubert had actually decided to call these four pieces a sonata, would we have thought any less highly of them? Though the first piece is generally thought to have insufficient impulse to form the first movement of a sonata, the vast opening movement of the great G major Sonata has even less. Yet, meditative though it is, it clearly forms the start of a great work, not least in Sviatoslav Richter's almost static recording of it.

Quite apart from that, however, the opening impromptu is a quintessential Schubert journey with the pianist as wanderer, upon whose transitory moods we eavesdrop. The second impromptu is a sort of scherzo in slow motion, complete with central trio section. The third is a theme and variations, akin to the andante of the A minor String Quartet and indeed based on the same theme from *Rosamunde*. The last is a stamping, syncopated dance, big enough to serve as counterweight to the first impromptu.

All very plausible, then – but the main argument against calling the result a sonata was that Schubert did not do so. He recognised the music as something different, though not necessarily slighter or less ambitious. The first piece takes its slowly circling major–minor contrasts of tonality far beyond anything in the *Moments Musicaux*, those nicely named Schubert miniatures with which the impromptus invite comparison, and it incorporates as second subject one of the most shimmeringly poignant of all Schubert's keyboard melodies. The second impromptu comes closer to being a *Moment Musical*, yet again its modulations – moving through two of Schubert's favourite flattened keys and then surprisingly into the more remote A major – go beyond what might be expected of such a piece.

The third, rooted in *Rosamunde*, is much too long to be considered a *Moment Musical*, and the last has that volatile, impatient, scale-obsessed quality that can make some of Schubert's seemingly more casual pieces end up sounding a lot less casual than at the start.

Among the innumerable complete recordings of Schubert's impromptus, Alfred Brendel's and Radu Lupu's are two of the most outstanding. Brendel's two-disc bargain-price set is notable for its poise, profundity and inclusion of the six *Moments Musicaux*, the three late *Klavierstücke*, D946, and two sets of German dances as a welcome bonus (Philips 456 061-2). Lupu's, also at bargain price, has impeccable beauty of line and clarity (Decca 460 975-2).

In comparison, the two-disc set by that perceptive Portuguese pianist, Maria João Pires, is not a bargain at all, and the title which has been bestowed on it, 'The Magnificent Journey', may seem superfluous. Yet this, in many ways, is the most enthralling and rewarding performance of them all, not least because the journey includes the mesmerising lilt of the little-known C minor Allegretto, D915, dating from between the two sets of impromptus. In addition, there is a poetic account, more spacious than Brendel's, of the three late piano pieces, D946, written just before the big B flat major Sonata in the last months of the composer's life (DG 457 550-2).

Fourteen

1827
PIANO TRIO IN E FLAT MAJOR, D929

Allegro   Andante con moto

Scherzo: Allegro moderato   Allegro moderato

In his great B flat major Piano Trio, it used to be said, Schubert achieved a perfection of structure he was unable to match in that work's even more ambitious and substantial successor in E flat major. But what Schumann would later hail as Schubert's 'heavenly lengths' have always seemed to some ears mere discursiveness, prompting one publisher to reject this work simply because it looked 'probably long' and the composer himself to make cuts in the finale which should never have been suggested to him.

Yet, whatever doubts Schubert may have felt about the size of the piece – Op. 100, as he himself numbered it – he was certainly by the age of 30 a hugely confident and original composer as well as a prolific one. His fecundity was phenomenal. His work-list fills twenty-six tightly packed pages in the *New Grove*. Ideas, indeed whole movements and half-completed works, were there to be cast aside if something more arresting suddenly occurred to him. But, in the case of the E flat Trio, mastery and maturity were present from first note to last. No movement, so far as we know, was discarded from it. Nothing deflected him from his task. It is a masterpiece on his grandest scale, as Schubert himself recognised.

Its fiercely chiselled opening bars instantly proclaim the explosiveness of his genius. And the identity of its first performers, who included two members of the famed Razumovsky Quartet as well as a distinguished Viennese pianist, suggests the quality of performance Schubert must have been aiming at when he completed it in November 1827, eight months after Beethoven's death and exactly a year before his own. The premiere on Boxing Day 1827 in the hall of the Vienna Music Society led to a further performance on 26 March 1828, when it formed the centrepiece of an important all-Schubert programme marking the anniversary of Beethoven's death.

Trying to trace Schubert's Beethoven connections can be a fruitless task. Though the two composers lived in the same city, and though Schubert (as the Berlin *Allgemeine Musikalische Zeitung* reported) was a torch-bearer at Beethoven's funeral, there is no hard evidence that they ever actually met. Nor was Schubert greatly influenced by Beethoven's music, however much he admired it, and however many authorities have called him a copycat. For the most part, he went his own way and explored his own distinctively personal world.

Indeed, as Alfred Brendel has sagely pointed out, Schubert did his utmost not to compose like Beethoven – which makes the so-called 'secret programme' behind the E flat Piano Trio all the more interesting. According to this theory, Schubert aimed from the start to make the work a posthumous tribute to Beethoven, written in the 'Eroica' key of E flat major, with an incisive 'Eroica'-like opening and with a trudging slow movement in the key (C minor) of Beethoven's *Marcia funebre*. Yet the effect is never Beethovenian, invariably Schubertian. This privately coded and entirely personal work is Schubert's 'commemoration of the death of a great man', to quote Beethoven's description of the 'Eroica'.

At the same time, it is music which is conspicuously forward-looking. The thrust with which the first movement is launched – the terse theme hammered out in octaves – shows why Schumann later compared it with an angry meteor 'blazing forth and outshining everything in the musical atmosphere of the time'.

A contrasting theme, softly tapped out in a different key, maintains the feeling of tonal instability which Schubert creates from the outset, though a third theme, beautifully sustained by the violin and cello, does at last bring a real sense of flow that continues into the development section. But here, as so often with Schubert, modulations render the beauty gradually more poignant and unworldly, more aware of its own sadness and mortality until, after a long build-up of tension, the home key and opening theme crash in again. Yet even at this point (in pedagogic terms the start of the recapitulation) the movement still has a long way to go, and we are reminded, as we listen to it, how the length of a Schubert first movement has doubled in size and eventfulness since the time of his early works.

The succeeding slow movement, marked *andante con moto* rather than the infinitely slower *adagio assai* of the 'Eroica', is one of Schubert's moody marches, with the piano providing a plodding *Winterreise*-like accompaniment to the dolefully ornamented melody voiced by the cello. Some experts claim this to have been based on a Swedish song entitled 'See, the sun is setting', which Schubert had heard performed in Vienna by the Swedish tenor Isaak Berg. In this context, however, it sounds utterly Schubertian, particularly when the piano plays it in high, bare octaves.

So where does the truth lie? It has taken one of the most probing Schubert scholars, Christopher Gibbs, to assert that the Swedish melody actually comes later in the movement, with a distinctive motive of a falling octave reflecting the words of the song at that point, 'Farewell! Farewell!' The fact that Gibbs is strong on the subject of the work's Beethoven link makes this *aperçu* all the more persuasive. As in many another Schubert slow movement, there comes a contrasted middle section in which thundering triplets bring emotion stormily to the boil, before some sort of morose peace is restored via the return of the main theme.

The contrapuntal scherzo is relentlessly animated, with a sturdily stamping middle section. This is the shortest of the four movements, whereas the finale is the longest, its sheer size in no way predicted by the charmingly airy melody with which it opens on the piano. Almost the entire movement is constructed out of this jaunty tune, along with the lightly pattering music that follows on the violin and cello, in what sounds like an imitation of the soft jangle of a Hungarian cimbalom – an instrument with horizontal strings struck by hand-held hammers.

For variety, there are characteristic changes of key, little dialogues and incidents, sudden upsurges of energy and, towards the end, a back-reference on the cello to the melancholy march theme of the slow movement – the sort of quotation which post-Schubertian composers would employ as a matter of routine (think of the finale of Dvořák's *New World* symphony and of Franck's Symphony in D minor) – but which in 1827 still bore the stamp of novelty. Those who accuse Schubert of long-windedness traditionally claim that this movement fails to hang together. Others may regard it as the perfect – and perfectly proportioned – completion of a cornucopian masterpiece.

Though the recording by the Beaux Arts Trio remains the classic modern version of this work, especially as the bargain-price two-disc set also includes the B flat major Trio (Philips 438 700-2), the more recent recording by the Florestan Trio is even more desirable. Not only does it catch the essential intimacy of this monumental work, but it includes as a pendant the full original version of the finale, enabling listeners to make up their own minds about its length. In a performance as committed as this, with Edinburgh-born Susan Tomes as the exhilarating pianist, a decision is easy to come to (Hyperion CDA67347).

Fifteen

1827
WINTERREISE, D911

Whether you call them song cycles or concert monodramas for voice and piano, Schubert's *Die schöne Müllerin* ('The Beautiful Maid of the Mill') and *Winterreise* ('Winter Journey') are his best 'operas'. In them he achieved the perfection of characterisation and scenic description, of narrative and dramatic timing, that constantly eluded him in his genuine theatre pieces. Each is a setting of poems by the Dessau-born librarian Wilhelm Müller. Each concerns a jilted lover. Each (but *Winterreise* especially) is substantial enough to fill an entire recital.

Yet, for all their similarity of style and subject, the one is no mere repeat of the other. *Die schöne Müllerin* is a rustic tragedy, filled with vignettes of country life, in which a miller's lad falls for his boss's daughter, loses her to a handsome huntsman, then drowns himself in the brook that has given the narrative its running background. The music is happy and hopeful, impulsive and ecstatic, as well as sad. Schubert was 26 when he wrote it.

Winterreise, dating from four years later, is its bleak, obsessive obverse. The story, consistently sombre and unfolded mostly in minor keys, starts near the point where the other ends. But this time, instead of killing himself, the forlorn lover stoically sets off on the 'winter journey' that gives the cycle its title. Everything he passes seems like a projection of his despair: the weather vane spinning on the roof of his sweetheart's house, the postman who brings no letters, the frost that whitens his hair as he walks, the snarling dogs, the bare lime tree, the inn that is really a graveyard, the frozen streams and other alienating symbols, until in the end he encounters a staggering, barefooted hurdy-gurdy man with whom he makes numbed contact.

The black, icy intensity of the music is relentlessly sustained, even through poems such as 'Frühlingstraum' ('Dream of Spring'), which may imply a momentary glimpse of sunshine but in fact do no such thing. Schubert himself thought them 'frightening' songs, adding that they had taken more out of him 'than was ever the case with other songs'. Dietrich Fischer-Dieskau, in his book on Schubert's songs, has asked whether *Winterreise*, as an 'intimate diary of a human soul', should be performed in public at all. Having sung it often, and recorded it six times, he naturally answered yes to his own question.

Yet, of all Schubert's songs, these as an entity are unquestionably the most disturbing and lacerating. The composer's friends were taken aback by their undeviating darkness of mood, and by the emotion with which Schubert himself sang them in private. Such music, said the sentimental and suicidal Johann Mayrhofer, confirmed that Schubert had been long and severely ill, and that 'winter was upon him'.

Elsewhere in Europe, winter was also upon the poet Wilhelm Müller. He died in September 1827 at the age of 32, just as Schubert, himself soon to die, was finishing *Winterreise*. The two men had neither met nor corresponded. Ironically, the seventy-seven poems that Müller assembled under the title of *Poems from the Posthumous Papers of an Itinerant Hornist* (the name a gloss on the already popular collection of folk poetry, *Youth's Magic Horn*, later to inspire Mahler) were dedicated to Weber, 'master of German song, as token of friendship and admiration'.

Weber never set them. Schubert came across them by chance. Müller, a minor but not negligible poet, had always hoped to find 'a congenial spirit' who would transform them into music, saying that they would otherwise lead 'only a half-life, a life on paper, black on white'. And though he never heard a note of *Winterreise* – and probably not of *Die schöne Müllerin* either – his hopes were bounteously fulfilled.

Schubert was not the only composer to find Müller to his taste. Ludwig Berger and Josef Klein, two little-known Germans of the period, also tackled *Die schöne Müllerin* (and Müller thanked Klein for his efforts). Brahms set two Müller poems. But nobody matched Schubert's zeal, whereby the *Winterreise* cycle was produced in two huge bursts of inspiration.

With *Die schöne Müllerin* behind him, his discovery of another dozen Müller poems in a four-year-old almanac must have seemed to him a godsend. These formed the first half of *Winterreise*, and he set to work on them in February 1827, writing 'finis' after the twelfth in the belief that there were no others. But later that year, after a mythical visit to Beethoven on his deathbed, he found that Müller had written a dozen more, and flung himself upon these as well. Though unaware of their intended sequence, he instinctively made his own musical sense out of them. If Müller's own (admittedly superior) final running order were observed, the Schubert Edition numbers would run 1–5, 13, 6–8, 14–21, 9–10, 23, 11–12, 22, 24. But singers who occasionally seek to honour Müller find that, in musical terms, Schubert's order works better. In song cycles, as in opera, the composer is the dramatist.

The first draft of the music was so feverishly written, and contained so many almost indecipherable corrections and second thoughts, that a fair copy had to be made by the publisher, who then gave it back to the composer to examine (so much for the traditional belief that Schubert could dash off a perfectly written song on the back of a menu). The final version, containing further alterations, was dated October 1827. The autograph of the cycle, published in facsimile, movingly provides visual evidence of the effort that went into composing it.

Through a characteristic interplay of minor and major keys, often in the course of a single song, and in music much of which moves at walking pace, Schubert vividly conveys the feelings of the embittered man on his lonely journey. In the opening 'Gute Nacht' ('Goodnight'), a last farewell is said to the house where the beloved lies sleeping; and the heart-wrenching move from minor to major at the point where the protagonist vows not to disturb her dreams sets the tone for everything that follows. In the second song, 'Die Wetterfahne' ('The Weathervane') whirls in the minor key, along with his anger.

But soon despair slows his progress. His tears freeze as they fall, and the piano's spiky detached chords in 'Gefror'ne Thränen' ('Frozen Tears'), said Gerald Moore in his book on Schubert's song cycles, should make the flesh cringe and the blood congeal. Minor keys dominate all these songs. But backward glances – to memories of rustling spring leaves in the major-key glow of 'Der Lindenbaum' ('The Lime Tree') – bring only renewed despair.

In 'Auf dem Flusse' ('On the River'), in music of extraordinary bareness, he scratches his beloved's name on the ice, minor moving to major as he does so. In 'Rückblick' ('Looking Back'), he frantically leaves the town where he had once been happy, and in the jerky music of 'Irrlicht' a will-o'-the-wisp leads him along the frozen bed of a stream into the mountains. He is now entirely alone, and when, in 'Rast' ('Rest'), he spends the night in a charcoal-burner's hut, he reports that his limbs cannot relax. In the lilting major-key music of 'Frühlingstraum' ('Dream of Spring'), he dreams of happier days, but harsh reality keeps intervening. In the terse minor-key music of 'Einsamkeit' ('Loneliness'), which brings the journey to its halfway point, calm, clear weather increases the storm in his heart.

Part Two begins with the false cheerfulness, in the 'Eroica' key of E flat major, of a posthorn. But this, as a minor-key intervention discloses, does not herald any letter from his beloved. False, too, is the illusion of age produced by the frost on his hair in 'Der greise Kopf' ('The Hoary Head'). Alas, too much of his life still lies ahead, with only the flapping wings of a crow ('Die Krähe') for companionship. By now, his grief and rage are steadily deranging him. The hostelry at which he halts in 'Das Wirthshaus' ('The Inn') is a graveyard whose 'rooms' turn out to be full. As he wanders on, he sees three suns in the winter sky, and it is then, with madness upon him, that he encounters 'Der Leiermann', the aged hurdy-gurdy man, playing a creaky, halting little minor-key tune above a drone bass. Together they disappear into the distance.

Like *Die schöne Müllerin*, *Winterreise* is a song cycle for tenor voice, though dark-toned baritones have understandably come to regard it as their exclusive property. Certainly, lightness of touch is not so much an issue here as it is in the more lyrical earlier cycle. Yet downward transposition does affect the sound of the music, not only in the vocal line but also in the piano part, which incorporates a degree of rumbling in the lower reaches of the keyboard. This is certainly avoided in Christophe Prégardien's 1996 recording, which is not only truthfully voiced by a tenor still young enough to be convincing but also has an accompanist, Andreas Steier, who makes the strongest possible case for the use of a Schubertian fortepiano in this music (Teldec 0630-18824-2).

If, on the other hand, a baritone and a modern concert grand seem to you to be essential features of this powerful cycle, then Dietrich Fischer-Dieskau and the Viennese pianist, Joerg Demus, remain unsurpassed exponents. In 1965, when the recording was made, the 40-year-old Fischer-Dieskau still sounded young enough to portray Schubert's shattered protagonist, and Demus's piano tone never booms (DG 447 421-2GOR).

Sixteen

1828
FANTASY IN F MINOR FOR PIANO DUET, D940

The title gives no real hint that this is one of Schubert's greatest works, the starting point of his last year, when one masterpiece followed another at uncanny speed. Though posterity has suggested he was aware his days were numbered, there is no more evidence of this than in previously productive years. He was simply by then in full command of his genius, capable of pitting himself against every challenge, and succeeding every time.

Nor was he invariably in a hurry. The F minor Fantasy, by Schubert's standards a shortish work which in most performances lasts less than twenty minutes, was begun in January 1828 but not completed until April and not performed (in private) until May, when the pianists were Schubert himself and his close friend and drinking companion, Franz Lachner.

Although by then he was within six months of his death, he was well enough in June to go on one of his excursions into the countryside outside

Vienna, with Lachner accompanying him. On the second day of the trip, they headed for Heiligenkreuz ('Holy Cross'), where there was a Cistercian monastery with a fine organ. Schubert proposed that each of them sit down and write a fugue to play on it. According to Lachner, the completed music was performed at midnight in the presence of a number of monks, and the two visitors set off again at six the following morning.

Not everything about Schubert's last year could therefore be described as harrowingly morbid. Writing of an existent piano version of Schubert's chromatic fugue, one of today's leading Schubert scholars, Brian Newbould, could not help remarking that, had Schubert lived as long a life as Beethoven, he 'might have seen *The Flying Dutchman*, *Tannhäuser* and *Lohengrin*'. In his last year, Schubert's music was in no way retrogressive but increasingly progressive, and progress meant, among other things, foretastes of Wagner.

Clearly, in spite of his doubtful health, Schubert in 1828 was looking ahead to 1829. To suggest that he prepared for his own death, and gave artistic shape to it, is something which, as Alfred Brendel has argued, belongs to the realms of fiction. Newbould's performing version of the last of Schubert's unfinished symphonies (labelled No. 10) supplies startling evidence of where he was heading. Schubert, as Brendel rightly declares, was 'in the middle of a magnificent process of musical evolution' when he died.

The F minor Fantasy certainly forms part of that process. Yet who could deny its whiff of death-consciousness? The question, of course, is whether it is about Schubert's own impending death or, more probably and more usually, about death in general. The combination of stoical sadness and at the same time of inexorable forward movement in the opening theme is utterly Schubertian and unforgettable. There is a moment towards the end of that disturbingly death-obsessed French film, *Betty Blue*, when we suddenly hear the quiet opening section of the F minor Fantasy on the soundtrack. The emotional effect it makes when it intrudes upon our consciousness is a reminder of the sheer power that Schubert's music possesses to hit us hard when unexpectedly heard out of context.

The music is like an intimately compressed version of the *Wanderer Fantasy* of five years earlier, written not for a single virtuoso but for two pianists seated side by side at a single keyboard. Virtuosity, in fact, is irrelevant to what Schubert has written here. Though clearly it requires two good players, capable of bringing a sense of climax to the closing fugue, this is an inward work in which feeling and perception matter more than flashing technique. The final moving reference to the opening theme is more important in this respect than the splendour of the fugue which precedes it.

Like the *Wanderer Fantasy*, the F minor is a sonata in disguise. Its four joined-up movements are based on the sort of thematic metamorphosis which would later capture Liszt's imagination and lead him to write his own hugely influential single-movement sonata. Again like the *Wanderer*, and many other Schubert works, it represents a journey in which the opening theme, with its typically 'walking' pulse, plays a crucial role. The whole first movement is devoted to it and to its troubled undercurrents, hovering between minor and major, darkness and light, the depths and heights of the keyboard.

The slow movement, pared to the bone, can seem little more than a series of grim trills and jerky, dislocated chords, with a soft, briefly yearning interlude – but its effect is bleak and deeply unsettling. The scherzo is a restless, rattling echo of the more jovial scherzo in the *Wanderer*, just as the finale, in which the theme from the very start of the work is gradually transformed into an inexorable fugue, also provides a sombre echo of things past. But Schubert has traversed a lot of ground in the five years that separate these fantasies. Here, the glitter of the previous work has been wholly suppressed; and when, in the closing bars, the opening theme is heard one last time, shadows descend on it as it recedes from view.

Schubert's F minor Fantasy shuns the cosiness of other four-handed music, and the better you get to know it the less cosy it seems. In this it differs from his other works of its kind, most of which – the *Marches Militaires*, the *Hungarian Divertissement*, the dancing *Ländler* – belong to the more convivial side of his musical nature.

Yet whether in seriousness or in jest, duets were a feature of Schubert's output which mattered to him. No other great composer produced them in such glorious abundance, and none wrote a 'Grand Duo' to compare with Schubert's in C major, D812. Dating from 1827, it is the vast major-key masterpiece – so ambitious in scale that it was once thought to be a piano arrangement of a symphony – of which the F minor Fantasy would become the terse and even greater minor-key obverse.

The recording which best captures its measure is the one by Radu Lupu and Murray Perahia, unhurried, rather stern, conveying the music's inner beauty without seductively turning on the charm. Coupled with Mozart's four-handed Sonata in D major, K448, it gives you quality rather than quantity for your money – forty-two minutes is not long for a full-price CD these days (Sony SK 39511).

If you object to this on principle, then go for Christoph Eschenbach and Justus Frantz, excellent, experienced duettists whose lavish survey of Schubert's four-handed music comes in a pair of two-disc bargain-price sets – four CDs in all. Their treatment of the F minor Fantasy, included in Volume Two along with the 'Grand Duo' and various shorter pieces, may be less searching than the phenomenal performance by Lupu and Perahia, but it is thoroughly Schubertian and more appropriately compiled (EMI 7243 5 69770 2 0).

Seventeen

1828
PIANO SONATA IN A MAJOR, D959

Allegro   Andantino

Scherzo: Allegro vivace   Rondo: Allegretto

It was a nineteenth-century belief, held by Schumann and others, that Schubert's last three piano sonatas represented a decline in his inspiration. Death was approaching. Schubert was under pressure – his own pressure – to complete what he had still to write. Something the same was said about Mozart during the last intensely productive months of his life, when *La clemenza di Tito* was thought to be a pale shadow of previous operas (some people still cling to this falsehood). Even Verdi, at the end of a much longer career, was deemed to have run out of tunes by the time he reached *Falstaff*, and the dying Debussy to have grown sterile in his last instrumental works.

The list, indeed, is endless, and often patently ridiculous. Some composers, Sibelius famously, ran out of steam. Others did not – and there is every evidence that Schubert was on a high in 1828, producing work after work of conspicuous inventiveness. Even the unfinished Tenth Symphony, of which the musicologist Brian Newbould has made an enthralling performing version recorded by Sir Charles Mackerras and the Scottish Chamber Orchestra, points to new things. It is almost as if Mahler and Bruckner were already present in Vienna.

So, the last sonata triptych, with the A major, D959, as centrepiece, should not be examined for signs of burn-out. It is a sustained and integrated group of masterpieces comparable with Beethoven's last three sonatas or Mozart's last three symphonies. Like these works, Schubert's form a unity of contrasts, a deep Schubertian exploration of the nature of three specific keys. They are the summation of his skills in one particular area of his output, and they were completed, one after another, in September 1828, two months before his death.

Yet there is no hint of haste in the way he composed them. They are conceived on the grandest scale, in Schubert's most expanded, unhurried manner, although they contain – as so often with Schubert – an awareness of mortality, which more than any other composer he was able to convey simply through a sudden, shocking pause in the progress of a piece.

But, though his health was by then rapidly failing, he found time during this period to produce not only these sonatas but also his great string quintet (with one of his terrible moments of death-consciousness at the height of its slow movement) and some of his finest songs. In addition, he journeyed with three male friends on a walking trip to Haydn's grave at Eisenstadt. And, ill though he was, he attended a variety of convivial evenings with friends.

The long-held theory that Schubert was a home-spun pianist, capable of improvising endlessly meandering pieces at the keyboard, cuts little ice in the presence of works as precisely composed as the last of his several sonatas in the key of A. From the pounding chords of its opening summons – which, no mere call to attention, turns out to be the first movement's main theme and returns like a buttress at the very end of the work – the writing is not only in Schubert's most expansive vein but is also thoroughly thought through, every phrase balanced and counter-balanced, every statement answered without a moment of discursiveness.

Yet, although the work's four-movement structure has been called conventionally classical, Schubert springs innumerable surprises within it. The most extraordinary of these comes when the gently rocking main theme of the minor-key slow movement – music seemingly of the calmest, most trancelike Schubertian simplicity, though by no means conventionally harmonised – suddenly peters out and prompts what can only be called an explosion of surging rage. Such eruptions occur often enough in Schubert to be recognised for what they are, though never more violently than here. With its stormy scales, ferocious trills and hammering chords, it is a passage that puts paid once and for all to the belief that Schubert was the sunniest of composers, his works filled with contentment and goodwill.

Schubert's bad temper, as portrayed through his music, has been the subject of recent debate, and the A major sonata provides the last and most extreme example of it. After this flurry of fury, the slow movement uneasily calms down, and the original theme quietly returns in a more elaborate version. But the sonata's equilibrium has been shattered, and not even the gay little scherzo (with some nervy undercurrents) and the flowing serenity of the long finale – one of those heavenly, though often strenuous, not quite invariably amiable outpourings of pure melody – can dispel memories of the slow movement's emotional turmoil.

Since no Schubert sonata is more challenging than this, it is not surprising that few performers manage to meet all its mental and physical demands. Rudolf Serkin's magisterial recording from the 1960s being currently unavailable, Alfred Brendel (intellectual vigour), Radu Lupu (beauty of line) and Stephen Kovacevich (blistering intensity) are the safe choices, depending on where your priorities lie. The way in which Brendel feels his way into the great eruption at the heart of the slow movement is an object lesson in Schubertian (and Brendelian) suspense. His treatment of the finale, on the other hand, sounds too restless.

But Brendel's inclusion of the twelve *German Dances*, D783, and other shorter pieces is a wonderful plus point. Not only are they a perfect postscript to the long sonata, they are played with a luminous simplicity which is exactly right. Dance music was as endearing an aspect of Schubert's output as it was of Mozart's, and seldom a mere social obligation. But whereas Mozart's was written mostly for instrumental ensembles of one sort or another, Schubert's was designed primarily for himself to play on the piano at convivial gatherings. It seems never to have been a chore. He composed it because it came naturally to him and because he was good at it. The inspiration he poured into his sonatas also went, without condescension, into these tender and high-spirited pieces, and that is how Brendel plays them.

Happily, many chains of Schubert dances survive in print, more than enough to represent this sizeable side of his output. But, in music so often dependent on improvisation, much has presumably been lost. There is a charming story about a wedding waltz being passed from one generation of a family to the next until, in 1943, it reached the opportunistic ears of Richard Strauss, who wrote it down and arranged it, rather lushly, for piano solo. Tall tale or true? Maurice Brown, one of Schubert's better biographers, treated it seriously enough to incorporate the details, along with the tune itself, in his book on the composer.

Eighteen

1828
PIANO SONATA IN B FLAT MAJOR, D960

Molto moderato   Andante sostenuto

Scherzo: Allegro vivace con delicatezza   Allegro ma non troppo

In the autumn of 1828, a few weeks before his death at the age of 31, Schubert decided that his knowledge of musical theory needed to be improved. With this in mind, he arranged to take some lessons in fugue from Simon Sechter, a noted Viennese pedagogue who was later to become Anton Bruckner's teacher. Though the onset of Schubert's fatal illness prevented him from receiving more than one lesson, the fact that he considered a course of further education to be necessary at all provides touching insight into the lack of egoism in his musical make-up.

Perhaps the fugal passage he had deleted from the finale of his 'Great' C major Symphony, replacing it with a melody which was one of his most sublime strokes of genius, had made him feel (quite wrongly) that his counterpoint creaked. Perhaps the splendid fugue which had formed the climax of his recent F minor Fantasy for two pianists had been a struggle. Perhaps his ambitious E flat major Mass, composed in the summer of 1828, had filled him with fresh enthusiasm for polyphony.

Who can tell? But his modesty, at any rate, was reflected in one of his letters of the period, addressed to a Leipzig publisher, in which he wrote: 'I beg to inquire when the E flat Trio will at last appear. Is it that you do not yet know its opus number? It is Op. 100. I long for its appearance. I have composed, among other things, three sonatas for piano solo, which I should like to dedicate to Hummel. I have also set several songs by Heine of Hamburg, which have pleased extraordinarily here, and finally written a quintet for 2 violins, 1 viola and 2 cellos. I have played the sonatas in a number of places with much applause, but the quintet will be tried out only in the near future.'

All the works were major masterpieces. The three sonatas, composed as a triptych in September 1828 and not published until a decade after his death, culminated in this far-ranging sonata in B flat major. Schubert, though he lived in rooms without a piano, had been a pianist all his life, and one of his special pleasures lay in playing in the houses of friends. Something of that intimate feeling can pervade even his largest, most public works, and is present in the almost confidential opening theme of this sonata. Then, after a mysterious subterranean trill and a pause – trills and pauses are a vital feature of the first movement – the melody is repeated in a way that suggests immediately the spacious scale of Schubert's thought processes in this work.

What sounds like an increase in pace, achieved by doubling the number of notes in the accompaniment, leads to yet another, now more powerful statement of the opening theme, which then subsides by way of a very Schubertian modulation into the distant key of F sharp minor for the arrival of the second subject. The calm lines of the music now grow more agitated as Schubert's ideas take him from key to key. Even more than other Schubert sonatas, this one could be likened to a journey – and one whose duration is substantially increased if the first movement's exposition is repeated, as Schubert requested.

To repeat or not to repeat has become one of the work's bones of contention. Sviatoslav Richter memorably did it at the 1964 Edinburgh Festival, making the first movement last a trancelike twenty-five minutes as a result. Alfred Brendel never does it, though he thereby deprives us of a linking passage which incorporates the soft subterranean trill in an ominous new fortissimo version.

But what really matter are the three slow, hesitant, unworldly chords in C sharp minor which, whether the repeat is included or not, lead the way into the development section. Their effect, typical of Schubert, goes far beyond how they look on paper or sound in the hands of an imperceptive pianist. The same can be said for the moment when the main theme moves poignantly into the minor, another typical touch, employed with maximum eloquence. Then, with the reappearance of the trill, now restored to the utmost softness, the music regains the security of B flat major at the start of the recapitulation. A quiet reminiscence of the main theme brings the first portion of the journey to its close.

The slow movement in C sharp minor takes us further into the world of Schubertian stillness. The opening theme, intoned over a softly mesmerising rhythmic pattern, seems to stretch into infinity as it enigmatically rises and falls through some of Schubert's most haunting major–minor progressions. At length, however, the atmosphere clears and the music reaches a more mobile middle section, sung by the piano as if it were some instrumental Fischer-Dieskau. Then, after a characteristic one-bar pause, the vision fades and the murmuring opening music returns, the rhythmic patterns now subtly altered so as to sound smoother and perhaps less questioning.

The scherzo is a masterpiece of delicate brilliance, with an unexpected plunge into the darkness of B flat minor in the central trio section – one of those terrifying Schubertian intimations of mortality in which the music seems suddenly to disintegrate. The lightness of the finale likewise darkens from time to time. A recurring 'wrong-key' tune, first heard (in C minor) at the very beginning, a more flowing theme with a genially pattering accompaniment, and a sudden almost Beethovenian surge of dotted rhythms are the ingredients which – with a closing burst of energy at increased tempo – combine to bring Schubert at last to his destination.

Schubert's final sonata has inspired many memorable performances, some of them conspicuously slower or quicker than others. Three recordings of it stand out. Richter's, the slowest and most disturbing of them all, but with the most mercurial scherzo, should be in everyone's Schubert collection (Regis RRC 1049). Dating from 1972, it has at times a certain brittleness of tone but is an experience filled with deep Russian melancholy and the Schubertian ability, as Brendel once put it, to move like a sleepwalker along the edge of the abyss. The inclusion of the C minor Sonata, first of the three last masterpieces, is an outstanding bonus.

Brendel's latest recording of the B flat Sonata, part of a two-disc collection of live Schubert sonata performances, begins somewhat impatiently, or so it sounds; but the slow movement is wonderful, and the set as a whole is enthralling (Philips 456 573-2). It is Mitsuko Uchida, however, who gets to the heart of the matter in a performance filled with half-lights and uncanny undertones – the soft trills in the first movement are articulated as if from the grave, and the three C sharp minor chords are studies in suspense which have to be heard to be believed. The three probing *Klavierstücke* of the same period form the perfect pendant (Philips 456 572-2PH).

Nineteen

1828
STRING QUINTET IN C MAJOR, D956

Allegro ma non troppo   Adagio

Scherzo (presto) and trio (andante sostenuto)   Allegretto

All Schubert's works, it has been glibly said, are early works – even the great C major String Quintet, composed during his last burst of inspiration, just before his death at the age of 31. Yet, simply because Schubert poured out so much music while still supposedly 'immature', and because he was reputedly a more slapdash composer than the similarly precocious Mozart, it has proved easy for pedagogues to pick holes in his music. Thus we are told that Schubert did not find himself as a symphonist until almost too late, that his early string quartets are mere student exercises, and that his piano sonatas are weakened by their discursiveness and by the fact that they do not always lie comfortably beneath the fingers. Worst of all, his grasp of counterpoint was feeble.

Even his greatest works have not escaped such niggling criticism, whereby the C major String Quintet is faulted (by one of the composer's leading British biographers) because two pages of its first movement happen to repeat the previous two pages a tone lower. In the words of David Cairns, a critic who believes, refreshingly, that Schubert knew what he was doing, the traditional distance between what the music-lover experiences in Schubert's works, and what the expert discovers they lack, represents one of the most abject of musicology's many failures, 'a dreadful example of the knowledge that darkeneth counsel'.

Another misconception about Schubert, particularly relevant to this quintet, concerns what is traditionally claimed to be the joyousness of his music. Of course Schubert wrote happy music – but it is a happiness always aware of its own obverse, and there are times when it breeds, quite deliberately, its own destruction. In that respect, his choice of C major as the home key of his string quintet, as well as of his greatest symphony, is significant. If we think of this as a cloudless key – that of Mozart's 'Jupiter' symphony and Wagner's *Die Meistersinger* – then Schubert shatters that illusion on the very first page of his quintet.

The apparently simple tonic chord that opens the work dissolves into a discord that casts its shadow over everything that follows. In essence, this is what the whole quintet is about: an assault on the security of C major, maintained until the last note of the (almost) hour-long score, where Schubert, by adding a baleful D flat, suddenly lifts the music forward in time to the sound-world of Wagner's *Götterdämmerung* and of Hagen's summoning of his troops to the sound of the same pair of notes.

By the fourth bar of the first movement, Schubert's quintet is already reaching towards C minor; and, when C major is retrieved a bar later, the harmony of the opening theme has gained a fresh poignancy. Within six bars, then, Schubert has loaded his home key with a sense of anxiety of a sort it rarely has to bear and which can be sensed even by listeners with no harmonic training. The mood continues throughout the movement, though Schubert allows the odd shaft of sunlight to creep in, as when the first cello, in its upper register, introduces the second subject in E flat major, one of those Schubert melodies usually described as songlike, yet actually quite unlike any of his songs.

String quintets differ from string quartets in the way the extra instrument enriches their tone colour and shifts their centre of gravity. In Mozart's great series of string quintets, the extra viola in the middle register adds graininess and a Mozartian poignancy to the texture. In Schubert's solitary quintet, the extra cello gives the work its special dark sonority, with the first cello frequently treated as a melodic instrument or else reinforcing the second cello in the bass. A further feeling of ballast, as well as of tension, derives from the fact that there are very few bars in which all five instruments are not playing together or straining against each other – not even Brahms so heavily taxed his performers in this respect.

The fierce central section of the first movement is matched by a similarly fierce section at the heart of the Adagio. The latter movement, however, begins in E major with music of ethereal stillness. Initially, it is fashioned out of a long, flowing melody, sustained by the second violin, viola and first cello in harmony, while the second cello supplies a pizzicato bass and the first violin a delicate little counter-theme. But words hardly convey the effect of this soft introduction, one of the most haunting passages in all Schubert.

As the movement progresses, the music grows more powerfully contrapuntal and turbulent. Yet maybe its most expressive moment comes when all these fiery trills and triplets suddenly collapse. The sound dwindles to the utmost quietness, and in a series of interrupted silences we are brought face to face with one of Schubert's awe-inspiring and alarming visions of death. Eventually, there is an attempt to recapture the spirit of the soft opening; but the original sense of calm has been lost, and in the closing bars there is a brief, ominous plunge into F minor, threatening the calm of E major.

At the start of the scherzo, the home key of C major is robustly retrieved, but there is something demonic about the way Schubert here propels the bracing opening tune – at face value no more than one of his beguiling Viennese dances – on and on. The trio section takes us even further from the world of benign Austrian dance music. The speed slows to andante, the key switches to D flat major, and the music slides into mystical sonorities of a kind that Bruckner would produce some years later in his symphonies.

The finale is the movement about which Schubert scholars are most prone to be patronising. Sir Jack Westrup, for instance, disliked what he called its 'café-music' elements, and Arthur Hutchings considered it 'irresponsibly unworthy' of the rest of the work. Yet the music, surely, is precisely in keeping with everything that has led up to it. The opening theme in C minor, with its crunching Hungarian cross-rhythms, is a relentless attack on the home key of C major. The moments of respite, produced later by the so-called café tune, represent the kind of fleeting happiness that is vital to the philosophy of this work. The disquieting discord heard at the outset of the first movement is still with us. And in the coda, where Schubert manically increases the speed in two ferocious sweeps, the darkest moment is kept for the end, where the first violin hurtles up a scale and the two cellos abrasively trill on a discordant D flat – a note that overrides, even in the final bar, the key of C.

In listening to this work, we should feel less concerned about Schubert's reputed shortcomings as a contrapuntist – what he knew about counterpoint served him admirably, even if around this time he revealed a touching desire to take counterpoint lessons – than by the way the music seems so starkly to predict his death a few weeks later. Those who regard this as an idyllic work, and there are many who do so, are not experiencing its reality. Schubert himself never heard it performed. The premiere – of an abbreviated version – took place more than twenty years later.

There are many good recordings of Schubert's C major String Quintet, one of the best – by the Hollywood Quartet – being one of the oldest. With Schoenberg's *Transfigured Night* as something more than a mere makeweight, it is certainly a prime contender, though the old-fashioned mono recording may put some people off (Testament SBT 1031).

Among more recent versions, the Lindsays with Douglas Cummings (ASV CDDCA537) convey the music's inwardness, and the Emerson Quartet with Mstislav Rostropovich (DG 431 792-2GH) its relentlessness, to impressive effect. Recruiting a star cellist is not necessarily an advantage in a work so utterly dependent on fine ensemble playing, but Rostropovich does no damage. The ferocity of the Borodin Quartet's performance (Teldec 4509-94564-2) shatters any residual belief that Schubert was a dreamily lyrical composer, but my own favourite remains the Hollywood – along with an undimmed affection for the old Amadeus recording with William Pleeth, if you can track it down.

Twenty

1828
SCHWANENGESANG, D957

To call Schubert's *Schwanengesang* ('Swan Song') a song cycle, as people traditionally do, is to mislabel it. Unlike *Die schöne Müllerin* and *Winterreise* – which are true song cycles, the greatest of their kind – it was never meant to be a unity. It tells no story. It employs texts by three quite different poets. Its title was not chosen by Schubert himself, apt though it now seems. Indeed, there is no evidence that Schubert ever intended the fourteen songs to be intermingled, but there is ample evidence that he composed the seven Rellstab settings and the six by Heine as separate groups.

Yet, as generations of singers have confirmed, the songs of *Schwanengesang* – the title dated from after Schubert's death – hang together in a strange, arresting way. They are a young man's music, based on words by poets equally young, but they do not conceal the circumstances in which they were created by a composer soon to die: their sense of loss (or impending loss), of isolation, of alienation, of tension, shot through with sudden shafts of sweet longing, is unmistakable. These are the elements that unify them, however arbitrary their unity actually is. To say, as does one of Schubert's latest biographers, that 'Die Taubenpost' ('Pigeon Post'), the final song, 'does not fit easily in the collection', may be perfectly true; but the author shows a serious failure to recognise that its touching simplicity becomes all the more potent when it serves as a pendant to the horror of 'Der Doppelgänger' ('The Ghostly Double').

Moreover, Seidl's 'Die Taubenpost' proves the appropriate and ultimately logical outcome of 'Liebesbotschaft' ('Love's Message'), the first of the seven Rellstab settings which form the opening portion of *Schwanengesang*. It succeeds in bringing this non-song cycle full circle. In it, a carrier-pigeon takes tender messages to the beloved. In 'Liebesbotschaft', which is the last of all Schubert's many pictures of a rippling stream, a similar lover asks the water to carry the same greetings. Water imagery, whether bubbling or diaphanous or menacing, was as important to Schubert as it has been, in our own time, to Iris Murdoch in many of her novels. It haunts the songs of *Die schöne Müllerin*, and it crops up elsewhere, sometimes symbolising death (or, as some authorities now claim, Schubert's possibly dual or bisexual nature) but finding an obverse in the composer's numerous, often jaunty, equestrian songs, a fine specimen of which also occurs here.

The second Rellstab setting, 'Kriegers Ahnung' ('Warrior's Premonition'), places amorous feelings in a starkly different picture, that of a military camp after lights-out. One soldier lies awake, longing for his beloved whom he fears he may never see again. It is the sort of text that appealed later to Mahler as well as Schubert, and indeed Schubert's setting is conspicuously forward-looking, its sound-world sombre, deep, almost Wagnerian.

The next song, 'Frühlingssehnsucht' ('Spring Longing'), returns us to rippling water, though here sunshine does nothing to dispel feelings of restless uncertainty. Indeed, in spite of the exhilarating pace, the sense of Schubertian longing increases. In such a context, the very familiar strains of 'Ständchen' ('Serenade') gain a fresh yearning, demonstrating that *Schwanengesang* works better as a song set than as fourteen individual songs.

Passion intensifies in 'Aufenthalt' ('Resting Place') as the music whirls through a wild landscape of raging torrents and stubborn rocks. In spite of the much slower pace of 'In der Ferne' ('Far Away'), the throb of the piano sustains the mood of the previous song until, with a switch from minor to major, balm is softly poured over the final section of the music. Then, in 'Abschied' ('Farewell'), the last of the Rellstab settings, robust cheerfulness banishes care. In this spirited equestrian song, the singer is riding out of town, waving to his forsaken girlfriends at their windows. This is the antithesis of the opening song of *Winterreise*, where the wretched lover trudges past the dark windows of his beloved's house. Yet it is not without its ambiguities. What are the implications of the abrupt modulations? Are his high spirits too good to be true? The music keeps us guessing.

The next song sweeps these questions aside, for it evokes a very different sort of traveller with the aid of the poetry of a very different sort of poet – 'that Heine from Hamburg', as Schubert erroneously called him. In 'Der Atlas' ('Atlas') the music staggers beneath the weight of the world. Anticipations of Wagner here grow more explicit. 'Ihr Bild' ('Her Likeness'), a bleak, slow-moving portrayal of loss, is followed by 'Das Fischermädchen' ('The Fisher Maiden') an interlude in the form of a fleetly rocking barcarolle.

Neither of these songs fully prepares us for the impact of 'Die Stadt' ('The Town'), an almost Debussy-like vision of a town viewed from a boat, 'where my beloved was lost to me'. The sea in 'Am Meer' ('By the Sea') is made equally ghostly through Schubert's obsessed use of keyboard *tremolandi*, all the more remarkable when we remember that Schubert was a composer who never saw the sea.

But it is in 'Der Doppelgänger', the last of the Heine settings, that the desperate climax of *Schwanengesang* is reached. The music of Schubert's 'double' or 'mirror image', representing perhaps his awareness of his own duality, seems to be conveying some grim, private message, all the more profound because it is delivered in the key of B minor – a key Schubert employed sparingly, but always (as in the 'Unfinished' symphony) to special emotional effect. Everything in 'Der Doppelgänger' lies in the music's atmosphere, not in its melodic line. In fact, there is no real melodic line; and its absence, in a song dating from so early in the nineteenth century, speaks eloquently for itself.

Compared with this, 'Die Taubenpost' – 'a simple love song, Schubert's very last', as one authority has succinctly put it – may seem too slight to be sung in the same context. Yet it has its own quiet pain and its own relevant point of climax when it reaches the words 'love's yearning'. It is a song as vital to *Schwanengesang*, and to Schubert's ultimately desolate philosophy, as those which precede it.

For a tenor recording of these fourteen songs, look no further than Peter Schreier's with Andras Schiff as pianist – two minds wholly in tune with Schubert's (Decca 425 612-2DH). The pianist Graham Johnson, in the last disc in his complete Schubert edition, divides the songs between two tenors, Anthony Rolfe Johnson and John Mark Ainsley, an interesting, not un-Schubertian idea (Hyperion CDJ 33037). If you prefer a baritone voice in *Schwanengesang*, then go for the exemplary Dietrich Fischer-Dieskau and Gerald Moore, not least because their three-disc bargain-price set includes *Die schöne Müllerin* and *Winterreise* (EMI CMS5 66146-2).

On 31 October 1828, Franz Schubert became unwell while having supper in one of his hostelries, but was well enough to go with his brother on a three-hour walk four days later. Next day, he had the first of what was intended to be a series of counterpoint lessons with Simon Sechter, but backed out of the next. A few nights later, he dined with friends, and was evidently in good spirits. Plans for his next opera were discussed with Franz Lachner, but by 17 November he was delirious and hallucinating about Beethoven. He died, aged 31, on 19 November at three in the afternoon. The funeral service was held two days later at St Joseph's, Margereten, and he was buried, as he had wanted, at Wahring Cemetery close to Beethoven, whose funeral he had attended the previous year. A memorial service was held at the Augustiner Church in central Vienna on 23 December, followed by a wake at the house of his friend Josef von Spaun.

FURTHER LISTENING

Though often described as a 'free thinker', Schubert composed religious music throughout his life, from a boyhood Salve Regina to the E flat major Mass he composed in the last summer of his life. Though none of these works could be called 'crucial' in the same way as his song cycles or his greatest symphonies and sonatas, the best of them are worth exploring. Here, as a pendant to the rest of this book, is a short note on the last of his six masses.

1828
MASS IN E FLAT MAJOR, D950

Kyrie   Gloria   Credo   Sanctus   Benedictus   Agnus Dei

Schubert's masses, after his operas, remain the most neglected – and the most frequently maligned – area of his output. Record-collectors have access to them; concert-goers too often do not. Yet the sixth and last of these works, the Mass in E flat major, dates from the last months of his life, the period that produced the great C major string quintet, the last three piano sonatas, and the *Schwanengesang* settings. Is it really so inferior to these masterpieces that it deserves to be wholly passed over?

If you think of Schubert principally as a writer of songs, symphonies, string quartets and piano sonatas, then you may indeed assume his sacred music to be an irrelevance. But in fact it represents just one more manifestation of his genius, and one that shows him approaching the subject of the Latin Mass in his own individual way, editing, cutting and responding to the text to suit his own feelings about God.

As a Viennese who never travelled far from home, he was clearly well acquainted with Austria's sacred music, as represented by Haydn, Mozart and Beethoven. When he made his decision, shortly before his death, to take counterpoint lessons from Simon Sechter, the likelihood was that he was planning to write more choral works. The E flat major Mass, indeed, surely provides the clue. It bursts with fugal writing in a way which his previous mass, No. 5 in A flat major, significantly does not. If he was considering an even more contrapuntal Mass No. 7, then some help from Sechter might have seemed sensible.

Not that the E flat major Mass is contrapuntally maladroit. The choral fugues come in the expected places, and splendidly sonorous they are. Indeed, they are more important than the music for the five solo voices which, by Schubert standards, may be thought unexpectedly reticent. But the true glory of this work lies in the orchestral writing, which is Schubertian through and through, from the first sweet tones of the opening Kyrie to the darker colours and final sense of uncertainty conveyed by the closing Agnus Dei.

The dramatic upsurges, the pounding drums and the sudden blazes of light are all as scrupulously calculated as the deliberate eschewing of flute tone. To hear this work reduced, as it often is, to the strains of no more than an organ accompaniment is to understand perhaps why it is so neglected in the concert hall.

Schubert's complete masses have been splendidly recorded on four discs by the Bavarian Radio Chorus and Symphony Orchestra conducted by Wolfgang Sawallisch with a starry array of soloists (EMI CMS7 64778-2). The E flat major Mass, drawn from the same recorded set, is also available as part of a two-disc recording, including the fourth and fifth masses (EMI CDZ5 73365-2).

FURTHER READING

Maurice J. E. Brown, *Schubert: A Critical Biography* (Macmillan, 1966)
Classic, enlightened, warm-hearted biography. Yet to be surpassed.

Christopher H. Gibbs (ed.), *The Cambridge Companion to Schubert* (Cambridge, 1997)
Excellent, up-to-date collection of essays for the serious Schubert-lover.

Elizabeth Norman McKay, *Franz Schubert: A Biography* (Oxford, 1996)
Thorough, unsensational modern biography by an acknowledged expert.

Brian Newbould, *Schubert: The Music and the Man* (Gollancz, 1997; California, 1999)
Famed for finishing Schubert's unfinished music, Newbould is one of the leading modern Schubert scholars. Though not the most elegant of writers, he gives us the facts in an always sympathetic, enlightened way.

John Reed, *The Master Musicians: Schubert* (Dent, 1987; Oxford, 2001)

One of a long-established series on the great composers. Life plus works, approachably presented.

John Reed, *The Schubert Song Companion* (Mandolin, 1997)

Comprehensive, blow-by-blow study of the songs, treated in alphabetical order. Endlessly useful guidebook.

Susan Youens, *Schubert's Poets and the Making of Lieder* (Cambridge, 1996)

The men who inspired him, and how he responded to them. A fascinating study by a fine American scholar.

GLOSSARY

Accelerando. Italian musical term meaning 'growing faster'.

Adagio. Italian musical term meaning 'slow', often interpreted as very slow.

Allegro. Italian musical term meaning 'light' or 'fast'. But is an 'allegretto' (meaning, literally, 'a little allegro') slower or faster than allegro? The term is usually accepted as meaning slower, but is irritatingly ambiguous.

Andante. Italian musical term meaning 'at walking pace'. Schubert employed it frequently, in preference to adagio.

Andantino. Irritatingly ambiguous Italian musical term, usually taken to mean a little faster than andante, but which can also be interpreted as a little slower than andante.

Arpeggio. Chord whose notes are sounded not simultaneously but spread out, usually from the bottom note upwards.

Assai. Italian word for 'very'.

Barcarolle. Boating song, often with a lapping rhythm, associated with Venetian gondoliers.

Baritone. Relatively low male voice, pitched between tenor and bass.

Baroque. Musical adaptation of an architectural term meaning 'elaborate, heavy, twisting'. The baroque musical style, often (but not necessarily) grandly formal, flourished in the seventeenth and eighteenth centuries, reaching its summit in Bach before giving way to the classicism of Haydn and Mozart.

Coda. Italian word for 'tailpiece'. The closing section of a movement, upon which Beethoven and Schubert bestowed increasing dramatic importance.

Con brio. Italian musical term meaning 'with spirit'.

Con delicatezza. Italian musical term meaning 'with delicacy'.

Con fuoco. Italian musical term meaning 'with fire'.

Con moto. Italian musical term meaning 'with motion'.

Counterpoint. The combination of two or more melodies or musical figures in such a way that they make musical sense.

D. Abbreviated prefix referring to the Deutsch index of Schubert's works. Otto Erich Deutsch (1883–1967) was an Austrian scholar whose complete thematic catalogue provides the standard chronological reference numbers for Schubert's works, replacing previous, wildly misleading opus numbers. For Example, the Deutsch number for the String Quartet in A minor, originally known as Opus 29, is D804.

Dactylic. Metre based on the repetition of one long beat followed by two shorter ones.

Descant. Extra melodic line sung above a given melody. Often employed in hymn tunes.

Diminuendo. Italian word for 'growing gradually quieter'. Abbreviated to *dim* in musical terminology.

Divertimento. A piece of entertainment music, usually for a group of instruments (strings and/or wind), in several movements.

Fantasy. In Bach's time and earlier, an instrumental piece, often in several sections, involving the free play of the composer's contrapuntal imagination. By the time of Schubert and Schumann, the term had become more poeticised, yet Schubert preserved the contrapuntal element in the finales of his two great fantasies for solo piano.

Finale. The concluding movement of a work (e.g. symphony, string quartet, sonata) in several movements.

Fugue. A contrapuntal composition or movement, or section of a movement, in which a chosen group of instruments or voices enter successively in imitation of each other. But, as Bach demonstrated and Schubert confirmed in his two piano fantasies, fugues can be written equally successfully for keyboard.

Giusto. Italian musical term meaning 'strict'.

Impromptu. Short piece of music, usually for piano, and often suggestive (misleadingly) of improvisation. Particularly associated with Schubert, and later with Chopin.

Incidental music. Music written to provide interludes at key points in a spoken drama. Schubert's most famous incidental music (still extant) was for a now defunct play entitled *Rosamunde*.

Kapellmeister. German for 'chapel master', i.e. the musical director of a prince's chapel or court. Came to be a derogatory term ('kapell-meisterish') implying dull musical routine.

Ländler. Austrian dance with three beats in the bar, precursor of the Viennese waltz. Schubert composed many melodious examples for piano.

Larghetto. Italian musical term meaning 'slow and dignified', but not so slow as largo.

Lied. German for 'song', especially if based on good poetry and composed, with piano accompaniment, by Schubert, Schumann, Brahms, Hugo Wolf or Richard Strauss. As a result, the word came to mean, somewhat pretentiously, 'art-song'. Plural: *Lieder*.

Maestoso. Italian musical term meaning 'majestic'.

Mezzo-soprano. Female voice pitched midway between the soprano and contralto registers. Today the female contralto is an almost extinct species, most contraltos tending to push their voices upwards and call themselves mezzos.

Minuet. Dance in triple-time, used by Haydn, Mozart, Beethoven and Schubert as the third movement of a symphony, string quartet and other works. The contrasted middle section of a minuet was known as a trio, because there was a tradition for writing it in three-part harmony. As time passed, Beethoven and Schubert replaced minuet movements with the similar but faster-paced scherzo.

Moderato. Italian musical term meaning 'at moderate speed'.

Molto. Italian word for 'very'.

Non troppo. Italian musical term meaning 'not too much'.

Piano quintet. A work for piano with (usually) a quartet of strings, consisting traditionally of two violins, viola and cello. But Schubert's 'Trout' quintet is unusual in that it is scored for piano, violin, viola, cello and double bass.

Piano trio. From the time of Haydn and Mozart onwards, a work for piano, violin and cello, usually in several movements. Initially the piano was the main instrument, with the violin 'accompanying' and the cello as little more than a passenger. It was Beethoven who emancipated the cello and made the three instruments equally important. Schubert followed suit.

Pizzicato. Plucked note on a string instrument.

Poco. Italian word for 'a little, a bit'.

Polyphony. Greek word meaning 'many voices', i.e. the simultaneous sounding of different lines, melodies or notes. Synonymous with counterpoint.

Presto. Italian musical term meaning 'fast', often taken to mean as fast as possible (which would in fact be *prestissimo*).

Rondo form. Italian term for what was traditionally the spirited finale of a symphony, string quartet or sonata. The word refers to the fact that the opening theme or section of the movement keeps recurring, or coming 'round' again, thereby forming an essential part of the music's structure.

Scherzo. Italian word for 'joke'. From Haydn's time onwards, it tended to form the second or third movement of a four-movement symphony, string quartet or sonata, where a dance movement, usually a minuet, had tended to provide light relief from the more serious matter of the rest of the work. A scherzo was often quite simply a very fast, in some way humorous minuet, with a strong pulse and (as in a minuet) a contrasted central section known as a 'trio', before the opening section was repeated in abbreviated form.

Sonata. In Schubert's time, a work consisting of three or four carefully structured movements. A three-movement Schubert sonata usually has a slow movement enclosed between two faster ones. A four-movement sonata has an extra movement, of dancelike character.

Sonata form. Term describing the structure of what was usually the first movement of a sonata during the period particularly of Mozart, Beethoven and Schubert. Put simply, it consisted of an 'exposition', based on two or more contrasted themes, a 'development' section in which the material already heard is developed, broken up or tautened in various ways, a 'recapitulation' in which the introductory material is reassembled in something like its original form, and a 'coda' or tailpiece, which rounds the music off or brings it to some sort of closing climax.

Sonorities. Sounds, as made by instruments or voices, either alone or together.

Soprano. The highest female voice, ranging from middle C upwards.

Sostenuto. Italian musical term meaning 'sustained'.

String quartet. A work for four string players, traditionally two violins, viola and cello. Haydn perfected the form, to which Mozart, Beethoven and Schubert all made major contributions. A string quartet is also an ensemble which performs string quartets.

String quintet. As above, but with an extra player, selected by the composer. Mozart's quintets had a second viola. Schubert, in his solitary string quintet, preferred two cellos.

Symphony. Form of orchestral work in several movements, usually of an ambitious nature. Much favoured by Haydn (known as the 'father of the symphony'), Mozart, Beethoven and Schubert.

Tarantella. Italian dance with a racy, swinging beat. Named after the tarantula spider. To dance the tarantella, it was superstitiously believed, helped to lessen the effect of a poisonous bite.

Tenor. High male voice, much favoured by Schubert, many of whose songs have to be transposed downwards, sometimes to excessively gruff effect, if a baritone wishes to sing them.

Tremolando. Having the effect of a tremolo (see below).

Tremolo. Italian word for 'trembling'. The rapid 'trembling' repetition of a single note, or alternation between two notes.

Trill. Musical term for the rapid alternation of the written note and the note above. In keyboard terms it can be a way of sustaining the sound of a note.

Triplet. A group of three notes of equal duration, written where some other quantity of notes (perhaps just a single note) is implied by the time signature.

Vivace. Italian word for 'lively'.